Dr High Would Like To Review Your Medication

Roz Scribble

chimpmunkapublishing
the mental health publisher

Roz Scribble

All rights reserved, no part of this publication may be reproduced by any means, electronic, mechanical photocopying, documentary, film or in any other format without prior written permission of the publisher.

Published by
Chipmunkapublishing
United Kingdom

http://www.chipmunkapublishing.com

Copyright © **Roz Scribble**

ISBN 978-1-78382-301-7

About Chipmunkapublishing

Mental health books give a voice to writers with mental illness around the world. At Chipmunkapublishing we raise awareness of mental health and the stigma surrounding mental health problems by encouraging society to listen. We are documenting mental health literature as a genre so history does not forget the survivors and carers of people with mental illness and disabilities.

Dr High Would Like To Review Your Medication

Dedications

This Book is dedicated to my mother. Also Paul Tracey, John Byrne, Selwyn Johnston, London Art College, Aunt Diana, Vivek Rauthan and family, Omi, Queen B of Coffee, Kerry, Michael Perez and of course my other friends, mentors
and a special thanks to my adversaries without whom I would never have become so much more resourceful.

Roz Scribble

Dr High Would Like To Review Your Medication

Chapter 1: The End
Chapter 2: When Rock Bottom Is Glass
Chapter 3: Hotel Loon
Chapter 4: Will Passengers Kindly Make Their Way to The Gate
Chapter 5: Mad Pennies
Chapter 6: Diagnosis and Self Concept
Chapter 7: Making Music Mad
Chapter 8: Time Travel
Chapter 9: 85 Percent is Normal
Chapter 10: In The Maldives
Chapter 11: Diagnosis Criminal & The 8 Day Migraine
Chapter 12: The Out of Hours Phenomenon
Chapter 13: Self Harm From The Horse's Mouth
Chapter 14: The Beginning

Roz Scribble

Chapter 1: The End

My story begins at the point everything stopped. I was at University in London, studying Jewellery, Silversmithing and "allied crafts" (i.e. we can't afford stuff) having completed Art College and graduating from that part of one's anatomy people refer to as the end of nowhere.

I was at that time looking forward to completing year two of the degree and hoping to set up shop with some Artist friends. Given that I was so shy I could barely make eye contact with Car Headlights I'm not quite sure where this confident business woman was supposed to emerge from.

My day would begin with the arduous journey of a sweaty and cramped trek on London's beloved Northern Line Rush Hour, forced intimately against a pinstriped suit and brown leather briefcase, trying desperately to avoid the unpredictable waggles of a ubiquitous City-Sized black umbrella. CS. I bet it had CS on the label too.

After a day there, I'd fasten myself inside the tube from East End to The West End, sleepily trudging past the buskers and the cave like echo of ancient guitar strings and saxophonists, through endless tunnels and out into the streets.

Negotiating the crowds along Charring Cross Road I'd pass the Big Issue Salesman near Leicester Square, who was 40 years my senior yet convinced I was in love with him.

Dr High Would Like To Review Your Medication

Roz Scribble

Chapter 1: The End

Approaching the Nightclub where I Bar Tended in Soho, I'd greet everyone, including the cloakroom girl who had more body piercings than an entire constellation. She made me blush by showing me some of her more intimate tattoos.

I had one discreet tongue ring, though another girl's husband complained that his wife was beginning to look like a chest of drawers.

Eventually, inhaling the familiar aroma of hot dogs and bus fumes I'd drag my feet to Trafalgar Square and sleepily lurch in rhythm with the Bus Driver's hand movements on his wheel.

Back south of the Thames I'd grab a couple of hours sleep, only to begin the same routine the following day. All while observing the correct Tube Etiquette, naturally.

That translates as pretend to read, busy oneself with a phone. But do not under any circumstances make eye contact with any sentient being, especially if he declares the entire carriage "Sinners". I approached such a man to ask for a flyer, just to see what would happen. He didn't give me a flyer, but he did give me a flat out refusal, so at least I didn't go home empty handed.

Saturday nights. After a 12 hour shift, one of my house mates would put on rave music of cataclysmic decibels approximately ten minutes after I'd hit the hay. Perfect!

Dr High Would Like To Review Your Medication

Roz Scribble

Chapter 1: The End

There were only another 20 minutes or so to go until my stop. I gave thought to some visual imagery in my mind's eye, deciding to ride out the rush and see if I would feel more relaxed once amongst familiar faces.

I was pretty certain it was a pending panic attack, as my mother had once raced me to A&E with similar sensations, much to their annoyance, and had been prescribed whatever the latest fad in antidepressants and beta-blockers. So I made an error of judgement in my assumption I could handle it.

Fourteen years old. My mind briefly wandered back to those days. I had known I'd be living in London by the time I was 17 or 18, just like many other kids stuck in miserable commuter belt areas. In fact I'd pretty much decided that by the time I was six. Of course I had based my decision on Films with happy endings.

I knew I'd make friends easily enough. I just didn't realise that these friends weren't ready for me, or I wasn't ready for them, actually probably maybe most likely both.

The train decelerated into another Tube Stop. Another mass scramble of people attempted to assert themselves and their possessions into a tolerable space. Another multitude of long, black umbrellas wedged in the closing sliding doors, as their owners desperately yanked and wiggled and squeezed the twiggy remains inside of the carriage.

Then another stab of adrenaline as I was wrenched back into the present and the trembling in my knees was now spreading all over my body and my teeth began to chatter.

Dr High Would Like To Review Your Medication

Roz Scribble

Chapter 1: The End

It hadn't occurred to me at the time that the majority of the passengers were extremely strung out too.

Like many people, and being the runt of the litter I had always felt the odd one out, especially at school. How I *hated* school. But that's another story.

Well, perhaps in part my long overdue parents' divorce had released a sense of crippling oppression in me once my father had moved back to Belfast, resulting in a suspicion of anything representative of authority. Perhaps it was the creatively stifling atmosphere of the school I and my twin sister had an "Assisted Place" at, compared to the state schools we were used to. Perhaps I was bored and direction-less, attempting to cope until I could apply to Art College back in the days when we still had grants.

Perhaps it was many, many things all combined, including the crippling and now accelerating anxiety I had felt regularly since my memories began.

I wasn't a bad kid. I was well behaved up until 14 years old. I was just a typically resourceless teenager struggling to make sense of it all with friends that just got drunk all the time and who were too old for me anyway.

And of course I was attempting to grow up way too fast which inevitably backfired.

Everyone remembers their last day at school. I remember changing into my Rock Chick clothes and escaping to a bar. To think I'd been so studious until I became a teenager and was released from the grip of my father.

Roz Scribble

Chapter 1: The End

My Tube Station would be arriving soon, or more accurately, I would be arriving at The Tube Station soon.

Shaking all over I attempted to grab my giant heavy toolbox and stand up. It was virtually impossible and other passengers began to notice my panic now, which only served to enhance it. I was just about capable of Minding The Gap, then caught in a rip-tip of fellow urban dwellers entered the rip-tide towards the staircase leading to the exit.

Over an hour's commute and with the entire number of letters memorised to form every single Station on the Northern Line I had been hoping for an ease in my impending panic by now. But it was getting worse.

1 stair, 2 stairs, and 3 stairs. My legs felt like lead and I looked at the daylight above thinking, "I'm never going to make it".

I realise to someone who has never had a panic attack in public I sound utterly ridiculous. But if it has never happened to you consider yourself lucky. My arms had stopped working by now. I dropped my tool box and fell. Not down the stairs but onto my backside. I sat there as a swarm of people tripped and trod on me. I just love that bystander effect.

No recollection of making it home. I just knew something in me went "ENOUGH!"

I locked every door and window, closed all the curtains. I had officially given up.
I sat smoking a rolled cigarette wondering what the hell I was going to do.

Dr High Would Like To Review Your Medication

Chapter 2: When Rock Bottom is Glass

Let us back track a little.

We are travelling back through time to the couple of years leading up to The End.

I was standing in the Nightclub where I worked. It was rock night, creatively titled "Club Rock".

Hundreds of people were performing their usual routine of waving twenty pound notes at me as if it would somehow make them look more conspicuous than everybody else.
I turned wearily towards the nearest person, aching from head to toe and he hanging a little too far over the line, as in *my line.*

"I'll have my usual", he slurred.

I looked at him with twisty eyebrows. Did he genuinely expect me to recognise him from all the other thousands of punters we had approaching the main bar week after week? What's more, his "usual" was nothing more than a pint of lager in a plastic cup.

We had a strict policy of not accepting 50 pound notes due the sheer number of counterfeits in circulation. As usual I attempted to explain over the rib shattering noise to one guy that I was sorry, no 50's allowed. Well this gentleman went absolutely nuts.

"I'M going to Complain to YOUR boss!" He screamed, storming off into the crowd.
Oops! It was Roger Daltrey.

I grew up around famous musicians (no I don't name drop, I suspect people that do are desperately trying to appear interesting). My Dad was a Professional Session Musician working with major Artists and TV with his own various jazz bands so I really wasn't fazed. Anyway, as that old Hot-Dog Vendor joke finishes. "Change comes from within".

Dr High Would Like To Review Your Medication

Roz Scribble

Chapter 2: When Rock Bottom Is Glass

I was as shattered as a Bus Stop on a Saturday night, after the 13 year old kids had been thrown out of the Nightclubs. I was too agoraphobic to walk to even a tiny grocer's. I gave up forcing myself to eat the plain boiled rice I had stocked up on and was dehydrated and malnourished. My weight plummeted to around 7 stone, and I'm fairly tall.

I haven't yet mentioned my house sharers in all of this.

One, when he wasn't up to his eyeballs on cocaine was reasonable company. He was a cashier in a music shop, having rejected his wealthy parents through upper-class guilt. I wish I'd been able to help him with his own identity issues. But young and naive, I thought he was going to kill someone before long. I didn't want it to be me.

The other lad was nice. He banged on about his A-level Film Studies too much and claimed that animals flocked to greet his mother. But hey, who am I to talk about delusions?

I did "nutty" things...

For example falling asleep on public transport but some reason would get a lift home from a passing paramedic. I guess I was lucky, *mostly.* I lost my keys so many times they got tired of me breaking in. I'd scale the side of the house and enter a bedroom, assuming he was out clubbing. Oops, in bed he'd leap out of it as if I'd arrived to "Collect some debts".

Dr High Would Like To Review Your Medication

Roz Scribble

Chapter 2: When Rock Bottom Is Glass

I know I'd passed my Goth phase. Definitely my Glam Rock phase, my Punk phase. I'd departed my hippy phase, and my Grunge phase. I did not follow Pop Music. I think I was in limbo music-wise. I eventually paid little attention to what I was wearing.

My twin once actually described my clothing as looking as if I'd got it from a Jumble-sale, at around 3:30pm, after all the best stuff had gone.

I do remember that I'd suddenly started listening to some Bill Evans, Frank Zappa and The Mahavishnu Orchestra.

I was fascinated by chords, taught myself piano scales off the back of a magazine (hence why I still use the incorrect fingering sometimes). I loved messing around with Jazz Chords by sticking an extra note here or there to see what effect the discord had on the chord sequence.

I bought a Sampler and a Drum Machine from one of my house mates. (Worst money I ever spent).

You could probably form some Pseudo-Scientific Graph detailing my mental decline by the increasing number of holes in my tights.

Still doing the Bar Gig, more holes appeared as I recklessly dragged them on. Should I walk to the Tube via the Market where I'd get screamed sexual abuse by the men on the Butchers Stall? Or jump out of my skin at the Cat Calls from upstairs at the Post Office? I did the latter, as at least I couldn't see them. So many species on the planet with so many splendid and sophisticated mating rituals, and we humans got the Wolf Whistle.

Dr High Would Like To Review Your Medication

Chapter 2: When Rock Bottom Is Glass

"The End" would be approaching within a matter of months but for the time being I just struggled on, unaware that one day in my future I would learn to figure out my own thought experiments to change the way I experienced life's challenges and certainly unaware of the difference between things I could change and CBMC's (Circumstances beyond my control).

I wasn't ready for the pressures of University life back then and there were certain things I found horrifying. Mostly I found Tooting a friendly place and my "local" was a lovely friendly Pub of Citizen Smith fame.

Yet I saw a Supermarket Security Guard get slashed with a knife and people standing around laughing. I saw a woman getting mugged at night from a distance and felt retrospective guilt for doing nothing. I was chased by some pervert on the underground. I was stalked by a guy. I had "a problem" with a taxi driver who wasn't a taxi driver after all. My house mates were nonchalant about it all. Alone in my fears, I eventually imposed a curfew on myself.

Skip Raiding with a friend for stained glass in the East End with a friend one day I got rather a nasty cut. As we looked for a place to patch me up we got kicked out of venue after venue, they didn't want my blood everywhere. We made a final attempt at a small pub, where upon entry we were immediately greeted by the sight of a topless woman on a decrepit pool table having coins thrown at her. She was worth less than a pint?

About turn!

Dr High Would Like To Review Your Medication

Chapter 2: When Rock Bottom Is Glass

The machinery in the foundry at University made me edgy. One day I would find the recording studio at Music College did likewise.

If it's my own equipment I'm fearless but the thought of breaking something and making it impossible for other people to finish their assignments?

And that is really where the way we think about the world pivots isn't it? The mere thought of it.

For anyone who has never really sat down (or stood up if you prefer) and considered it, what generally happens in your mind when you are feeling really bad? You are thinking, of course. But what many people don't consider is *how* we are thinking and what happens to our thoughts, feelings and emotions.

Imagine a bad time you've had and a good time. Thoughts translate into feelings, and into behaviour. If the situation runs as a film with special effects and surround sound, rather than little pictures, that can make the feelings stronger. What do you see and hear? Are you prophetic regarding what might happen next and then end up *feeling* worse?

Once I yelled myself awake, and the neighbour's dogs, and then their neighbour's dogs. I inadvertently orchestrated an entire neighbourhood symphony of variable barking sounds at around 4am, and only because of a bad dream, causing me to wake my entire neighbourhood.

Dr High Would Like To Review Your Medication

Chapter 2: When Rock Bottom Is Glass

We are always in some kind of trance. We are abstract and metaphorical by nature. We spot something that jogs memories. We don't relive the true memory, we relive the way we represent the memory. As when we do as we are imagining something challenging next week, such as having a job interview, and so on.

Whether it's our shopping list trance or our 'I'll never be able to cope with meeting all these strangers' trance, something sets our thoughts off on another trajectory.

We see a car similar to one our ex-partner used to drive and depending on how we remember them, using our 5 senses *inside* our minds this time, we suddenly feel great, or really terrible.

At night we may think about the things that keep us awake. We are in an "awake" trance. We are hypnotising ourselves to stay awake. But when we realise the alarm will alarm us in 20 minutes, we reverse those thoughts and focus on how tired we are, and suddenly are aware how tired we are.

I played a game with this idea. Every time a bad memory of someone arrived, I switched it to a memory of us enjoying ourselves. Within less than a week this happened without needing to try.

Unless of course it's a CBMC in which case there is absolutely nothing you can do and it's better to move to the next chapter and see where life goes next, which is exactly what we are going to do right now.

Dr High Would Like To Review Your Medication

Roz Scribble

Chapter 3: Hotel Loon

My self-harm (or what I prefer to call my negative coping strategy) escalated to the point that I had a fight with a full length mirror, banged my head repeatedly against a wall and cut up my arms.

Blurred memories... Some people, turning up at my house.

My house mates kept well out of the way and I somehow found myself in an Enormous decrepit Mental Hospital in South London.

The staff didn't really acknowledge me in the first 48 hours. It became clear I was now a number and the staff didn't care, so I needed to make allies and fast.

It was about 3am during the first night and I was doing my best to ignore the spider on the ceiling directly above my bed. I could hear laughter coming from the day room. I made a bold move. *(Deep Breath.)*

I slowly opened the door from the Women's Dormitory and saw a bunch of men and women having the best laugh I'd seen in a long time. A true example of connectivity when people are trying to survive in the same boat, and they clearly could see the funny side of their predicament.

I tip-toed closer with the trepidation of a hermit crab auditioning for a Rock Band and a tall guy with a glass eye waved me over.

"Oh 'ello!!'OO are you den? Come on over luv. 'Ave a ciggie and a seat!!!!!"

I had found my people.

Dr High Would Like To Review Your Medication

Roz Scribble

Chapter 3: Hotel Loon

The morning shift staff arrived, battle ready, to drag everyone out of bed and looked especially surprised to see me, the newbie sitting up with people and a little bit annoyed that the kitchen staff had forgotten to lock up hence the used and empty tea cups all over the place.

They dragged me off to drug me and weigh me as it was assumed I was anorexic apparently when I wasn't. I was just on the Scared-of-Shopping diet, though I began gaining weight even with no food over the first few days just from the horrible Drugs and doing nothing.

I think I did get briefly interviewed by a junior doctor who just wanted to know if I intended to harm myself or anyone else.

I rolled my eyes.

Some people *will insist* on reading certain tabloids that run weekly nonsense stories on Schizophrenia and machetes and supermarkets. Because everyone needs a hobby *right*?!

There was no "Therapy". Table-Tennis! (Brilliant! Great for cabin fever.). A boring TV I could not be bothered with. Nothing else, no books, nothing to do.

So generally unless the ward was unlocked and we could all escape and go for an adventure it could be a little dull, but there was such a mix of people of all ages and backgrounds they became my new family.

Dr High Would Like To Review Your Medication

Chapter 3: Hotel Loon

There was a diverse range of issues.

I didn't take any death threats seriously simply because nobody else did. And everybody had bad days followed by especially bad days. I felt terrible for people would thought they could hear commands in their head because I could see so clearly the level of distress and panic, these deeply embedded lines of terror in their faces.

Eventually a stern looking nurse approached me, folded arms.

"Doctor High would like to review your medication."

Um. Uh. Ha!! I couldn't stop smiling.
I did that thing one attempts to do with one's face to prevent laughter but it didn't help, and the nurse was becoming increasingly angry.
I doubled over and roared with laughter.

"Dr...Dr...Dr... Pffffffftttt!!"

I was marched into a room full of people, silent and serious people with clip boards.

"Are you Anorexic?" asked Dr High.

"No."

"Okay, you may leave."

(That was weird. Obviously he wasn't paid by the word.)

Dr High Would Like To Review Your Medication

Chapter 3: Hotel Loon

One of the ladies I met in there kept cuddling me and wrapping me up in a filthy blanket. One guy convinced himself I was his run-away bride and he had come to fetch me, to go to his home country. (Catatonic Schizophrenia, apparently.) Another guy was blind and I got some great insights from him about that.

One day he decided he was a Shaman. Now I'm admittedly unacquainted with Shamanism. Shameful, but I'm pretty sure it doesn't involve smashing the glass to the Nurses Station with a White Stick, making "Whooooooosh" noises.

Oh, an elderly lady had faecal incontinence all over my bed. As I fetched clean sheets a nurse started screaming "This isn't a bloody Hotel you know!" (A repetitious and commonplace remark amongst the staff, which increased with tedium over time). As usual she didn't believe a word I said so I insisted she took a look. Only then was I reluctantly allowed to change my sheets.

All in all though, I felt pretty safe. No crossing the road as people approached. No carrying keys on my fingers in case I was attacked. No placing a curfew on myself to be home by dark. But some of the staff was not good. I've met one or two pretty unethical people in recent years, but some of these took the biscuit and slammed the crumbs back in your face. I was groped by a member of the higher ranks, but didn't say.
Who would believe a "Nutter"?

Dr High Would Like To Review Your Medication

Roz Scribble

Chapter 3: Hotel Loon

It's not all fun and games in a giant old decrepit Mental Hospital.

I remember one poor guy becoming so tormented by the voices in his head he stuck his head through a tough double glazed window.

I had some incidents myself, usually triggered by false accusations or unnecessary anger on the part of the staff, which led me to smashing glass and attacking myself. I was extremely fortunate that some butterfly plasters and bandages avoided the need for stitches. I'm going to address self harming much later as I was simply accused of attention seeking which is an opinion worthy only of pity and ridicule.

A woman on one side of my bed had regular panic attacks that literally floored her. She simply couldn't stand or control her limbs at all. And the poor girl in the bed on the other side of me kept escaping but making very scary attempts to die. One night she was dragged in by half a dozen police officers and the staff ripped down her jeans, a syringe was produced and she was heavily sedated. She had stitches from ear to ear from where she had attempted to slice her own throat.

Then I got news that my father had suddenly arrived in England and was staying at my mother's house when I hadn't heard from him in 10 years.

Why?!

Dr High Would Like To Review Your Medication

Roz Scribble

Chapter 3: Hotel Loon

We had a few marbles lying around, but not enough for everyone. (Yes there is a joke in there but it's so obvious I'll let you figure it out). So what did the nice tall friendly guy with the glass eye do? He *removed* his glass eye. There! Enough for everyone. That, ladies and gentlemen is generosity in action!

Other times I would come out of the Dormitory wondering why it was beginning to look a lot like Christmas. Ahhh! I knew who was at it again. It wasn't his fault. This young man had tragically severe special needs and was in the wrong environment for his needs. But after raiding the laundry room, there stood the halls, decked with bras and knickers.

Sometimes we would be placed on a Bus for "Loony Outings". I only remember one, a trip to Brighton. Not wildly exciting as before those days, I used to sleep with friends on Brighton Beach, with a nice campfire and spend the weekends Nightclubbing. It must have looked pretty odd for people to see Rock Chicks getting washed and dressed in the public toilets on Brighton Pier

Everyone was sunbathing during this "Loony Outing". Sunbathing makes me want to scream with boredom so I just went swimming, fully clothed.

Often though I remember we would organise our own adventures and sneak out during evening shift change. I had no idea the extent to which we were so notorious around Tooting for it, until one of the barmen in The Kings Head asked after my Psychiatrist.

Dr High Would Like To Review Your Medication

Chapter 3: Hotel Loon

I begged the staff to ban my father from coming anywhere near me and he did comply. For now I would have to wait and see because as usual all family information was withheld from me.

Most people that came to visit me there were furious more than anything else. My twin who was back from Galway briefly said the first thing that entered her head was "What have they done with my sister?!"

Most people had similar reactions. I had disappeared under a haze of drugs and not much of my personality remained. They were very old fashioned drugs (as today's will be in 5 or 10 years) and I was "Zombified". I was putting on weight too fast even for an inpatient or inactive person but when eventually, in the future I got online I researched medications a great deal. I wanted to learn everything I could about Psychiatric medicine, even emailing researchers and asking them for PDFs.

Because pills don't cause weight gain, right? Lots of things cause weight gain. How we eat food is one aspect. I challenge anyone who thinks anti-psychotic medication doesn't cause weight gain to take anything that suppresses Dopamine because it *does* affect the Pituitary Gland thereby increasing levels of Prolactin, a growth steroid present mostly during adolescence and pregnancy. It can even make men grow mammaries and lactate.

This is extremely old news now but it was denied for a very long time.

Dr High Would Like To Review Your Medication

Roz Scribble

Chapter 3: Hotel Loon

Summer moved on and so did some of the patients, to halfway houses, or chronic wards. Some became homeless. Some had families that wanted them back.

One of my house mates visited to inform me I was now homeless, but then I struck gold. A fantastic friend of mine from my Bar Work days and her boyfriend were looking for a flat mate and liked Tooting as you could see more sky than the forest of Tower Blocks they lived in.

So it was settled! I didn't have to go to a Half Way House after all and I would be sharing a flat with one of those rare gems you meet in life that you feel really lucky to be friends with. We didn't know what was happening until one evening a woman I internally referred to as Nurse Ratchet began squawking at me.

(She honestly communicated in squawk talk).

"What the HELL do you think YOU are doing here?" She squawked.

On she went. I have a habit when people yell at me of going deaf and recalling none of the verbiage. It's genuinely not deliberate, it's just fear I suppose. I'm sure some neurologists out there know the causality. I just sat there in stunned silence having not a clue what she was shouting at me for.

It turned out I had been discharged that morning and nobody had thought to tell me. So I packed my things and cringing beyond belief,

I walked all the way back to the house I'd just been kicked out of. It was that, or sleep rough.

Roz Scribble

Chapter 4: Will Passengers Make Their Way to the Gate

Let's get back to Tooting.

This time it was going to be different. I would get well... somehow and be the best flat mate ever invented. My dear friend even talked about us all getting out of London and heading over to Dublin.

She and her guy were great. It's a rare shell on a sandy beach to find a friend that doesn't leave you intellectually thirsty afterwards. And I tried, so, so hard.

But really, I needed more care. I wasn't going to get that in a heavily over populated town near Brixton. The day hospital was boredom on a stick. My one perk, getting nicknamed 'The Artist', a label I've always shied away from due to compliments making me blush. But that was a way to pass the days, sketching people. It sure beat cooking biscuits.

There is an old word Psychiatric Professionals love to use called 'Catastrophising'. It's very common if one simply must label absolutely everything and I've met so many people that do it who have never ever been near Psychiatric Services. More commonly 'Catastrophising' is a fluffy word for making a mountain out of a molehill. And it was everywhere at the Day Hospital.

For example a client would bake cookies but they would come out as a sort of wafer thin cake. And you could see the bottom lip quiver as it clearly meant something far more enfeebling for their self worth.

Dr High Would Like To Review Your Medication

Roz Scribble

Chapter 4: Will Passengers Make Their Way to the Gate

I thought I was going to be attacked.

I wasn't convinced, but the *feeling* was it would be a man and he would be very loud as he repeatedly stabbed me. I sat at home in silent darkness, tears pouring down my face waiting for a sound, any sound to let me know he or they were approaching.

I had witnessed a stabbing and a mugging. I'd been stalked and chased and these experiences built into a general sense of incredible danger and trauma.

I had my really bad days too of course in "The Day Hospital of Relentless Tedium" as I silently named it. Many days, knowing I could help myself if only I knew what to do and how to do it and frustrated from the knowledge that I lacked that necessary skills to help myself.

I really wanted to be a good flatmate as I said. I just couldn't take any more. So one afternoon I swallowed all of my medication. It wasn't my only overdose. It's just that only some them were actual suicide attempts. The others weren't "cries for help either". Nor "Attention Seeking". Help from whom for what? There wasn't anyone I'd met that even knew how.

I just needed to *STOP* the terrible thoughts. Thoughts, so terrifying, it was as if I could inadvertently cut myself on my very own ideas. (That is a metaphor before someone decides to name it and put it in the next DSM). So I had to halt my thinking immediately in the most resourceless way imaginable.

Dr High Would Like To Review Your Medication

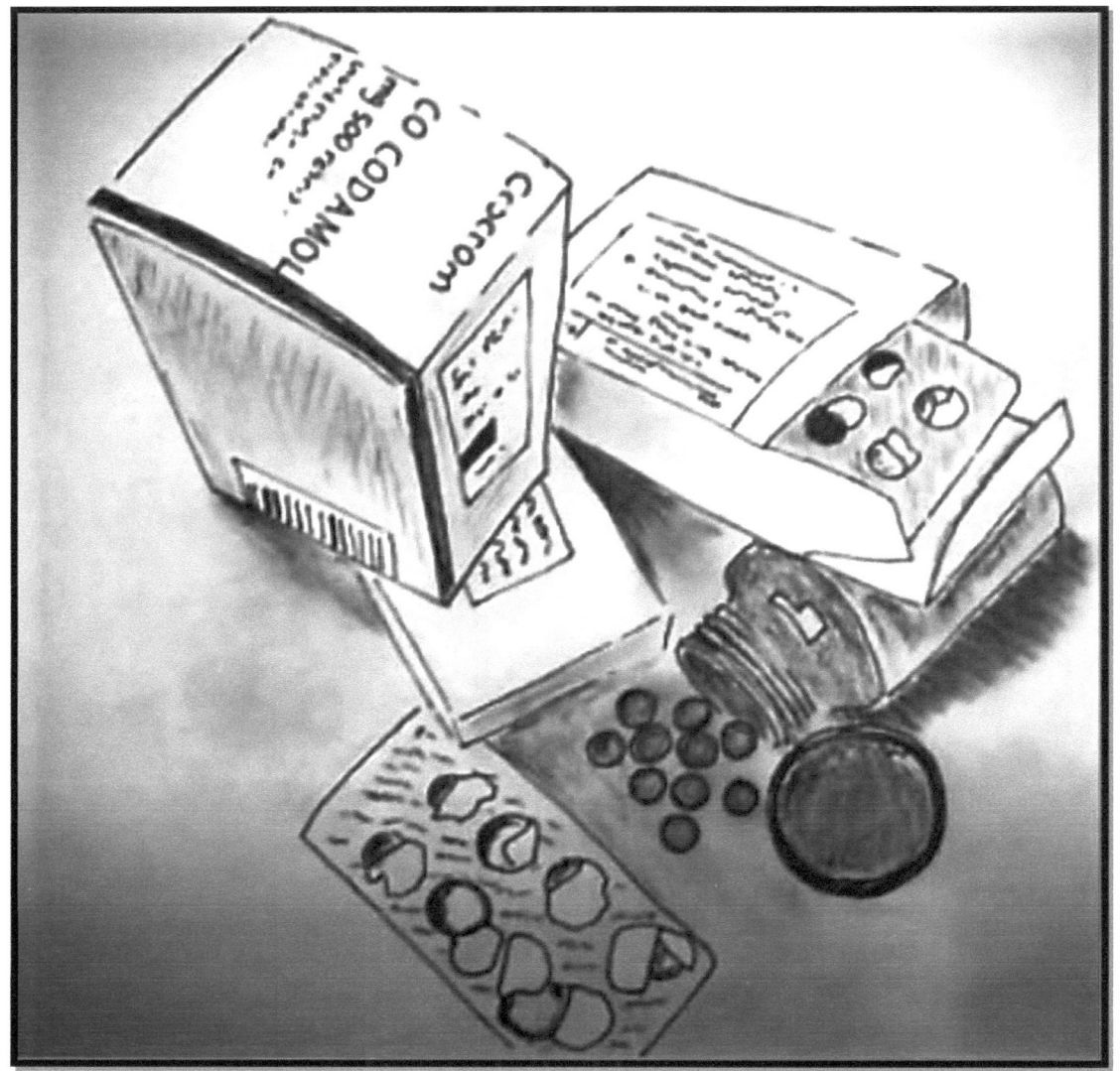

Roz Scribble

Chapter 4: Will Passengers Make Their way to the Gate

Poor friends! My Girl found me and dialled 999. She must have been told not to let me fall asleep because as my memories faded and everything became distorted and confusing I collapsed. I heard a distorted voice say "Oh No You Don't!" That is the last I remember. Her dragging me on my feet and making me try and try to walk.

Apparently I forgot everything about the world after that. I couldn't tell the ambulance guys my name or date of birth or answer any questions at all. I woke up three or four days later in the cardiac unit and holy fish, my actual *Dad* was sitting there!

It had been a long, long time. He dealt with everything using comedy. He always had when he was being compassionate. He had already had a quadruple bypass and 4 heart attacks so his inappropriateness had me giggling.

"Your monitor shows some pretty strange arrhythmia but you have a strong pulse, you'll live. Not like him."

He gestured across the room. "He's eff yoo cee kayed". Typical dad. I was suddenly glad he was there, though concerned for the guy across the room! He told me they had agreed to release me in a few days if I went to *his* and mums house. *(His* what?).

My mind State switched instantaneously to the negative.

Dr High Would Like To Review Your Medication

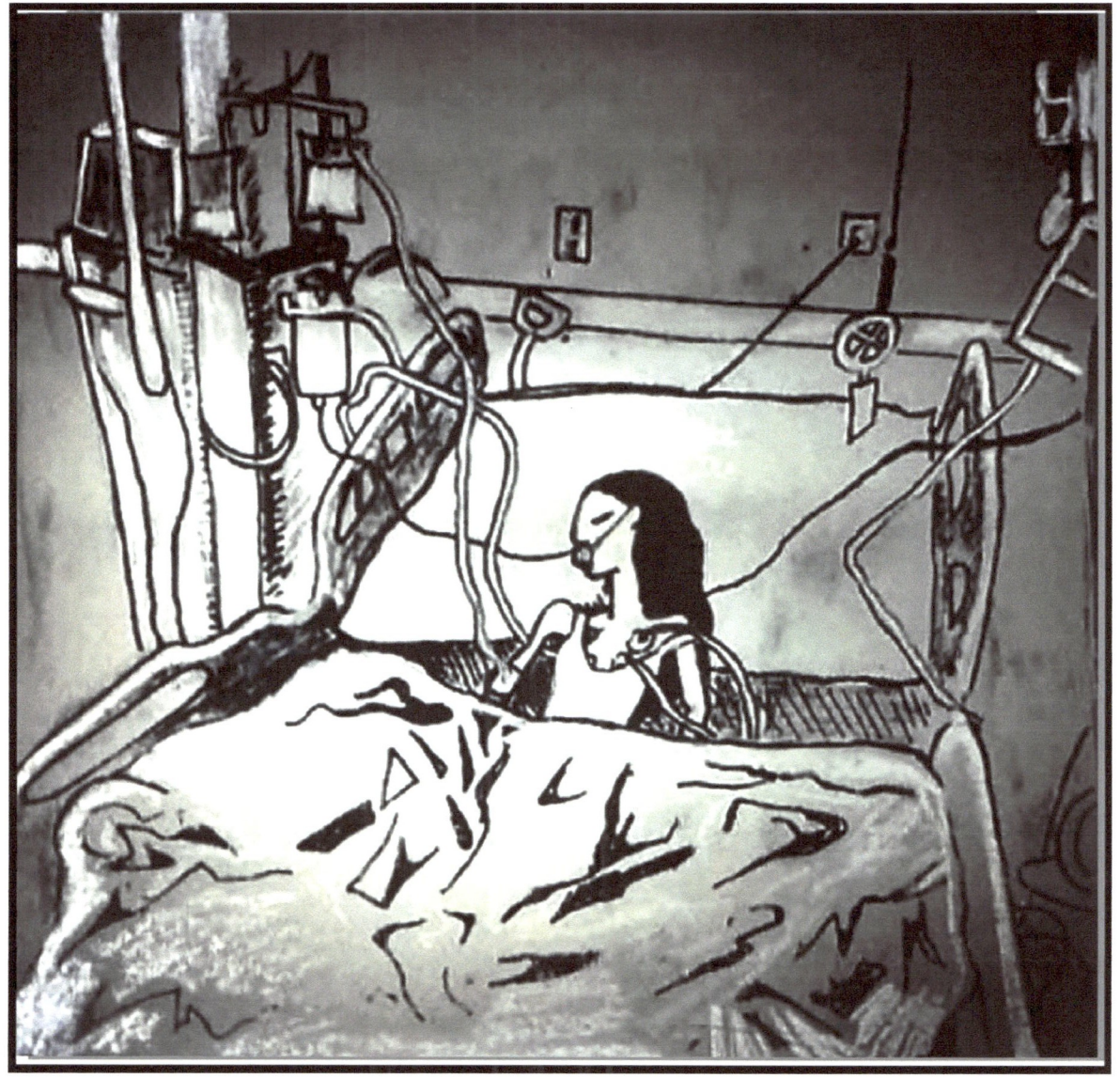

Roz Scribble

Chapter 4: Will Passengers Make Their Way to the Gate

So much for being the best flat mate ever. I was deeply sorry and they were so forgiving. I lived in limbo between London and that house for a while. I was furious regarding my parents reunion.

Worse, he announced that he hated England and was taking her to Belfast. My twin was meeting them there. I just had to accept it. Then I had a thought. Go with them. People thought I was running away. Hey guys. It was the best decision I ever made!

Fights continued. He'd announce he was leaving and never coming back, only to return 10 minutes later to find mum on the computer playing Tetris! He didn't realise that kind of thing has always been mums way of avoiding dealing with emotion. It wasn't personal.

The rest is a blur. I know I was sleeping in various different places including a Gypsy Camp and an enormous decrepit house where we Punk Rockers partied and I joined one of their bands on keys.

Strangely enough one School Biology Teacher lived there too, who we of course referred to as "Sir".

If only I'd known Psychiatry was but one Model, just maybe I could have taken some responsibility. I would, eventually when I realised if I wanted good answers to my questions I'd have to ask myself, then listen carefully.

Dr High Would Like To Review Your Medication

Chapter 4: Will Passengers Make Their Way to the Gate

I don't remember much else in the six months or so before moving to Belfast. It was like Ground Hog Day for a while, then we piled in the car to drive to Scotland to get the ferry. It was stuffed to the gills so that meant I spent most of the journey in the back upside down in the lotus position.

I do recall stopping at a service station, virtually empty save a couple of cleaning staff. My dad lost his temper over the only available food. A bowl of mushroom soup, which tasted more like what I imagine a Slug Casserole must be like. Not that anyone was around to hear him.

Eventually when we arrived on the ferry I just went to the bar. Six O' clock in the morning and I was the only girl in there but I was tired and needed space. Very Spaghetti Western. I don't think an entire bar has shut up and stared opened mouthed like that at me ever.

I was tempted to spit and announce that I was looking for the Sheriff but I tucked myself into the quietest spot I could find instead.

As we entered The Belfast Lough I felt the first stab of excitement in ages. A new life was about to begin and I had no idea, *(really* no idea) what was in store for me.

Dr High Would Like To Review Your Medication

Roz Scribble

Chapter 7: Mad Pennies

The first thing I noticed arriving in our home in the section of Belfast we were to reside was the rubble. Dereliction intertwined with roads of tiny terraced houses with eyeballs peeking out of the cracks in the curtains, wondering I suppose where my father suddenly had obtained a wife and 21 year old offspring. My twin, the comedian peeked right back... Well, not so much peeked at blatantly stared back. Our new neighbours would step back in slow motion in an effort to appear invisible. I think rubbing a spot on the window would have looked more innocent.

Bearing in mind that I was very, very unwell and doped up from middle C to the 88th note on the Piano with old fashioned Psych Meds, I was a little surprised. A kind of reverse multicultural shock. I was scared of people as I didn't see anyone with dark brown eyes like mine. I wondered what it must be like to be a black person moving to the area as I felt self conscious of my accent. I only saw white people. I really felt way out of my depth.

That isn't intended to be disrespectful at all. It was simply the brand new need to adjust to a totally new environment and being extremely unwell simultaneously. Of course in retrospect there was plenty of individuality amongst the folks in the area I eventually grew to feel comfortable by the friendliness of the people and decided never to return to London.

Dr High Would Like To Review Your Medication

Roz Scribble

Chapter 7: Mad Pennies

The Troubles were still somewhat alive and unwell and Belfast was yet to become a noticeably popular destination for immigration. We arrived a couple of months before the riots and bombs and hijackings. The "Good Friday Agreement" was yet to come, and there were still British Soldiers in packs of threes, scaling the streets and I was paranoid and ignorant regarding the complex history of Belfast despite all the books I had bought.

July arrived and the curfew was imposed. I recalled some of the people I used to know who frequently sipped red wine, languishing in describing London as a military state and wanted to slap the naivety right out of their powder- edged credit card stupidity. They had never seen a riot, yet were happy to slump drunkenly into an armchair half watching TV, half imposing on everyone else their dry and unworldly versions of "what's what".

Having said that, I soon read Orwell's 1984 and globally speaking the similarities filled me with a helpless feeling, as if being chained to the cliff edge of a precarious concept I saw as a crazy imposition of other very powerful people's delusions, encroaching upon my own apparently cheap and expendable existence.

Meanwhile we were living in a damp and cramped house and my father was losing it. Rage after rage. Screaming and yelling. I worshipped my twin in those days. Everything he spat she spat back to the point of making him speechless, and I attempted to follow her around like an adoring yet unwanted shadow.

Roz Scribble

Chapter 6: Mad Pennies

I diced with death with what I firmly determined would be the last OD I would ever take. I felt terribly guilty, especially with my mother.

Dad and the family piled themselves and I into a car, raced to the Hospital, stopping once as dad spotted a pal and hit the brakes to shoot the breeze and exchange some jokes and have a catch up. Poor mum was seething as I lay semi-conscious in the back. My blood pressured crashed by the time we got to A&E.
(This was all explained to me afterwards).

The poor staff tilted my bed in an attempt to allow gravity to get oxygen into my brain, the problem with that being that my lack of circulation caused my tongue to fall against the back of my throat and make breathing exceptionally difficult. I attempted to form words to a nurse, who scurried away in fear, never to be seen again.

After some time, I've no idea how long, I was placed in a wheelchair, into the back of a van and taken to the infamous Mental Hospital of terrified children's (and adult's) horror stories. Purdisburn, now known as Knockbracken.

Juxtapose severe relentless agitation with an environment as dynamic as a catatonic dog lying in the sun and you will get a glimpse into the amount of inaudible screaming going on in my head. I paced and paced and paced some more. I wondered if it was actually possible to die of boredom.

Dr High Would Like To Review Your Medication

Roz Scribble

Chapter 6: Mad Pennies

One day I *really* needed exercise. I became a stealth-like Wonder Woman as I sneaked right out of the grounds. Suddenly, the awareness struck me I was in trouble so I raced back, passing a couple of the girls in my ward.

"Hey! They're looking for you!"

"I'm heading back now!" Lungs at bursting point.

"We won't say anything!"

But I was supervised consistently after that.

After a week behaving carefully I demanded to see The Chief and to my amazement he reluctantly agreed to a 3 day trial release, not that my family wanted me back. Leaving, I could see where the actual roads had been on fire and upside down buses and cars, burnt out.

Mum had been house hunting franticly and struck lucky. Someone on the coast wanted a quick sale and due to house prices being so much lower she snapped up a place in a sleepy village by the sea. We threw our belongings into the car and moved in immediately with no furniture, but certain that it was going to be a real home. There was a little trouble in the village so in a very old Irish Pub they locked and bolted the front doors where the windows had already been nailed with wood and planks and kept the pub open. When people left they slipped surreptitiously out the back, as did we.

Dr High Would Like To Review Your Medication

Roz Scribble

Chapter 6: Diagnosis and Self Concept

Let's get back inside a Psychiatrist's office.

5 minutes, maybe? 10? I can't really remember how long it took the man with the crossed legs and the perpetual circular motion in his foot raised over the other to say the words.

"Well... You are Schizophrenic."

(What?!)

He was leaning back in his aerodynamically designed office chair behind a large wooden desk scattered with files toying with the button on a pen some Drugs Rep had given him, making a little too much eye contact as I looked back at him, speechless.

The representations in my mind's eye kept changing as I tried to come to terms with the "Word" and the flippant manner in which he had calmly handed me my new life.

I saw a Tombstone, I saw a community that I was observing from a distance, I saw a city as I walked through it, translucent. I saw the world as a spider's web of precarious networks and I had no idea what that all meant or what I was supposed to do with them.

The Psychiatrist directed a fixed stare into my eyes as if to say "This is non negotiable".

The doc went on to explain that Schizophrenics lack insight, have delusions and hallucinations and gave more examples that terrorised me into the assumption that I would 'catch' every one of them. That I would form the conviction people would be able to hear what I was thinking. ("Thought Broadcasting").

Dr High Would Like To Review Your Medication

Roz Scribble

Chapter 6: Diagnosis and Self Concept

He hadn't finished. Schizophrenics sometimes think people on TV, the Radio, in Songs were communicating directly to them. Paranoia was frequent, he reported. Thoughts that they were being followed, stared at, that people were watching the house and seeing things that weren't there. For example a bush could become a man with an axe, about to attack them. Hearing voices, commands too. Kiss that stranger! Go and steal that bread. Punch that person. Or clients would hear the voice of god in their head telling them they were going to hell. Smash that window. Walk along the middle of the road.

That I would spend my life on medications, in and out of hospital and never return to studying or work for the rest of my life.

Gee. Thanks, Nostradamus!

Oh my gosh. The change in my self-concept was horrendously seismic. And the girl that walked into that office left some kind of sub-species, or alien.

The thing that seems strangest to me now is that nobody asked me about this. Nobody asked what had changed when I was diagnosed. How it changed the way I saw myself, how I now felt about me.

And not one person asked how it affected my role or how I related to members of my family, my friends, my immediate environment, culturally, or the entire world and beyond. It never occurred to me to ask myself till years later studying numerous Therapeutic models myself.

Dr High Would Like To Review Your Medication

Roz Scribble

Chapter 6: Diagnosis and Self Concept

There is something very obvious I want to add.

No Doctor walks into a bay in a ward in Hospital and coughs, without really needing to clear his throat, only to say the following.
"Mr. Blogs. I'm sorry to inform you that you are a broken leg."

Any halfwit knows that a broken leg is not the sum total of a person's parts, and sorry Doc I have to inform you that your clinical diagnosis in the world of Mental [ill] Health isn't either. It is insanity itself to think otherwise.

R.D. Laign famously said, "The range of what we think and do is limited by what we fail to notice. And because we fail to notice that we fail to notice, there is little we can do to change; until we notice how failing to notice shapes our thoughts and deeds".

I was told that I *am* a Schizophrenic. Why partition us "crazies" off as if we are some separate species?

It is like "HELP! I got Ostracised!" So I ran fast and buried my head in the sand. PHEW!!!

I am a daughter, a sister, an artist, a Jeweller, an adventurer and above all a human being.

Roz Scribble

Chapter 6: Diagnosis and Self Concept

A good CBT practitioner (one of only a handful of therapists fully trained and accredited to work with people diagnosed with Psychosis in the UK) and I had many chats and he enlightened me with some wonderful insights, as this was his speciality.

People used to tell me that the difference between Neurosis and Psychosis was that Neurotics extremely exaggerate the truth or at least something plausible whereas Psychotics just conjure up nonsense that makes no sense with absolute conviction.

This is now exceptionally outdated thinking, and I mentioned to him that there was a part of myself that wasn't convinced whenever I experienced delusions so I could step back and examine the evidence with myself to some degree. He said that he had never had a client that had 100 percent convictions over their delusions, which really pleased me as he explained that modern mainstream therapy was trying to normalise psychosis so that it wasn't so different a category from OCD or PTSD. Too true, I absolutely agree.

It's great when I occasionally meet 'Normals'' who actually get it. And it always makes for intelligent and stimulating conversation.

Roz Scribble

Chapter 6: Diagnosis and Self Concept

It's equally great to meet open minded professionals who have the humility where they can acknowledge that they could never truly understand what it has been like in my life. And I can equally agree that I will never understand what it must be like for them.Chapter 6: Diagnosis and Self Concept
I don't fully understand what it is like to be a man, or to have been though childbirth (not the men of course!) But I could equally say that about "Mental Illness". Everyone's experience is different, and there is absolutely no line between well or ill. It is a spectrum, and we are all a little bit crazy!

We have our senses. These different senses, we use them to make *sense* of the world around us. We construct more abstract inner worlds that we live in alone on the inside. These are constantly coming into play but more so when an event happens to make our self concept change more dramatically. Very extreme events that alter the structure of how we relate to the world can have catastrophic effects on our self concepts, identities and personalities altogether.

What is it like to locate your self concept outside of this society?

These days there are people doing work to put greater research into this. It would be even greater if it was not only integrated into therapy and change work, but if understanding ourselves was as normal a part of keeping healthy as exercise. Maybe the point of intervention should be as important as exercise at school? Way before the trajectories we follow lead us to the point where our self concept is said to be Pathological. But for the time being. Without resources we are not educated in these important understandings until it's too late, and we are sat in a Psychiatrist's Office.

Dr High Would Like To Review Your Medication

Roz Scribble

Chapter 6: Diagnosis and Self Concept

Remember that people considered to be Psychotic are not ill all the time, just as 'Normals' are not rational all the time.

I remember someone once asking me to explain, or rather challenging me to explain, what it was like.

I replied to him that it was like having your drink spiked with a particularly nasty and frightening drug. One where you began tripping horribly. Only in this case, you had no knowledge at all when, or indeed if, it would ever wear off.

He pretty much began spluttering with rage as he attempted to process what I had just said. I remember he claimed that was simply impossible. It was too much! That nobody on Earth would be able to cope with that! You would just go mad!

"That!" (I was waving my arms in seething frustration by now), "is the exact bloody point!"

(It's all rather confusing for everyone isn't it?) I have made a promise to myself to work at this life. And to be much more gentle with people, even when I feel they have really hurt me. They haven't. I believe they are the trigger but the gun was pointing at me already. Because I have developed myself through my own life's events and it is how I form my identity, my vulnerabilities, my core beliefs and my self concept itself. The great thing is learning *how* to change. "A leopard can't change it's spots" people have said.

Well, I'm not a leopard!

Dr High Would Like To Review Your Medication

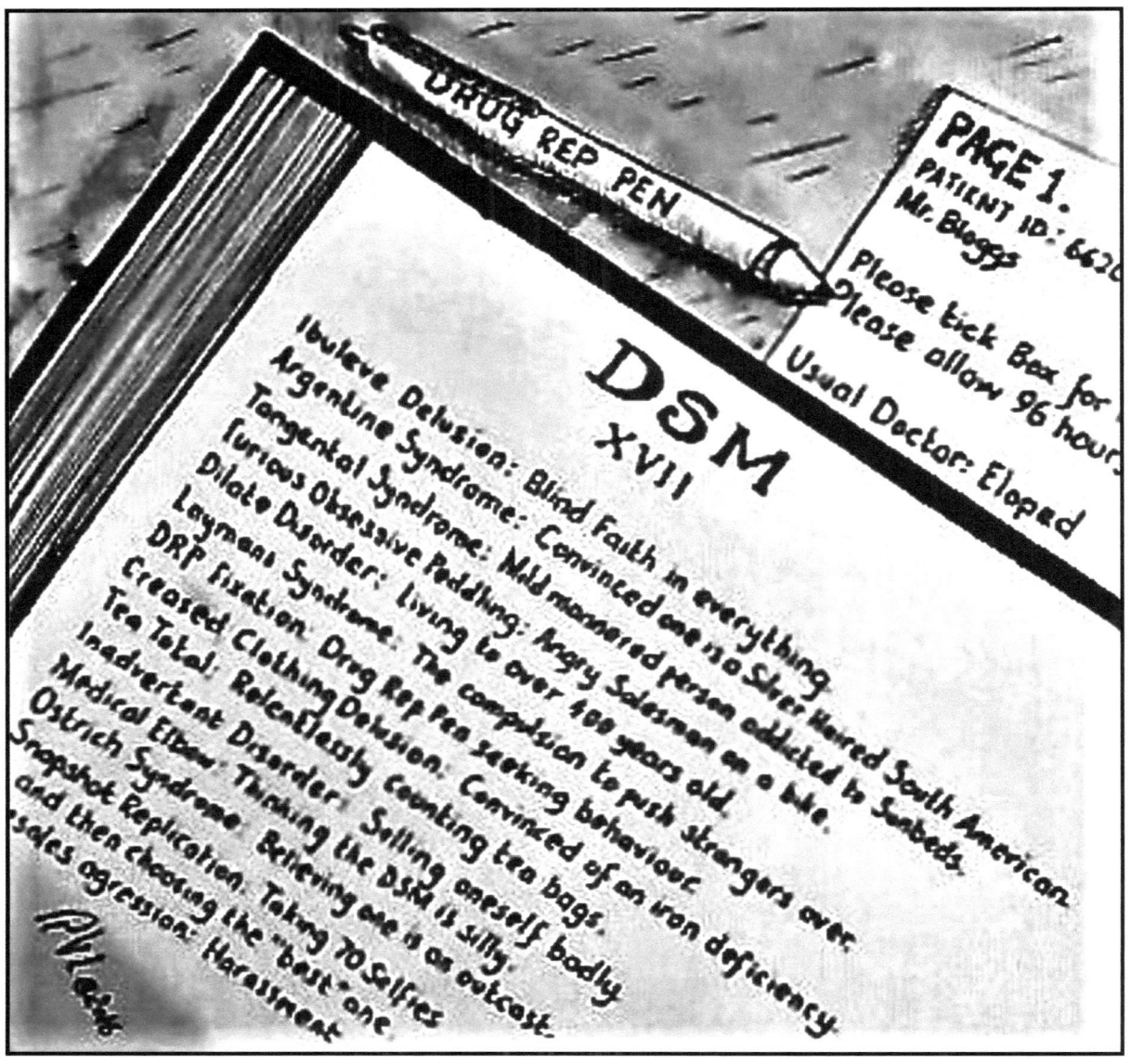

Roz Scribble

Chapter 7: Making Music Mad

My twin didn't stick around for long. She and Dad continued to yell at each other and Mum and I continued the pretence of affecting the mannerisms of wallpaper.

I met lots of his friends, all musicians of course including the couple I had first met in Belfast who played in a Jazz Quartet with Dad and I still consider them my good friends today.

After a while a Trumpet player my Dad played in a duo with came up with a great idea. Why don't I go and study music?

There was a college 7 miles away that had a music department and I could learn Jazz Piano and make some friends closer to my own age. He even bought me a Mountain bike, which I became addicted to and cycled 1 hour after college every day and then a good 14 or 15 miles along the pretty coastline at the weekend.

I was so terrified I was half drunk during the interview but they were so lovely and gave me an immediate yes and I didn't realise I had just met my new, actually my first real Mentor, a talented composer and he would remain so for the next 4 years.

Everyone I knew, except the Trumpet Player was in opposition of my decision. The Psychs and my CPN, My father (I think thought it was too "middle class" - just gig). But making music was never my only motivation. I wanted to meet people. I wanted to have something, just one thing I could call my own world. And it became so much more.

Dr High Would Like To Review Your Medication

Roz Scribble

Chapter 7: Making Music Mad

My attendance was bad for the first six months due to almost blind terror and then I made a picture in my head that I was going to damn well prove the whole world wrong, even if I crossed that finish line by crawling along the ground to the surprised open mouth of my crazy boss and handing in my final assignment by my breaking fingernails!

They could stick me in a straight-jacket and restraints and reach for the Anti-Psychotic Syringe afterwards for all I cared, fine, but not before.

And it was attempted to put me away a few times during those 4 years. Too bad. No room at the Loony Inn. Ner Ner-Ner Ner Ner! So I returned to my studies.

I was addicted. Sometimes I stayed there with my best friend, a wee lad with reams of talent who makes me burst with pride till half past nine at night, when I would get kicked out by the staff.

We studied everything from Music Theory to Recording, Engineering, Pre and Post Production. We studied Composition, Arranging and Orchestration. When performing we didn't just play some tune for the class. We had to Compose, find musicians, form a band, rehearse and book and promote venues. I got to hear about a whole new world of music out there and it was exceptionally empowering.

Roz Scribble

Chapter 7: Making Music Mad

Shock, horror and whispering! Two years in I began a relationship with one of the teachers and of course he wasn't allowed to teach any class I was involved in.

My Psychiatrist, who had been an Aunty to me, was crazier than I was. I mean livid. She said even apart from how unethical it was, anyone 10 years older than me, with dubious ideas about women forming a relationship not only with a student, but a vulnerable student who was legally disabled was taking a huge risk even by going there in the first place, was a waste of my time and would break my heart.

Stubborn me ignored her anyway. We were together for the next 3 years and it made studying much harder as I sat in my tiny flat crying my way through my assignments.

Hey though. "Him outdoors" wasn't all bad. It was a great learning curve and I chose to remember the happy and fun memories and forget what needs to be forgotten. I'd happily have a Ballygowan and chat about old times. I wasn't easy to be with either!

I cared about him a lot. I've dated but never settled down since.

Dr High Would Like To Review Your Medication

Roz Scribble

Chapter 8 - Making Music Mad

I did graduate. It was four of the best years of my life, that place. (Except Graduations. Boring! Even your own.)

I learnt a very important lesson. Who gives me permission to attempt the things I am passionate about. Me, that's who.
I'll give you a little tip by way of example, should anyone ever tell you you're not capable.

"You'd never be able to do that!"

Just say "Really, how do you know?"

And inevitably they will come up with some logical fallacy starting with "because..."

"Because you don't do stuff like that. You are more of an X person."

There is a difference between What, Why, and How.

People have asked me so many times am I a What or a Why person. I just shrug and say "neither.", and in the words of an old friend from Delhi I smile and confuse them.

I am a how person. Thank you mad-music, you taught me a life lesson.

Dr High Would Like To Review Your Medication

Roz Scribble

Chapter 8: Time Travel

Remember that Psychiatrist that gave me the long list of You-can't-because-you-are-a-Loon, and that I changed it to a to do list?

Well. A year after Making Music Mad Him Outdoors and I finally split for good. And like all good ex boyfriends I heard he was going around playing the victim and I needed some distance. Time to return to my to do list and start moving again.

I ran away to Vancouver, and Vancouver Island for 2 months. The idea was my uncle was going to be away and my Aunt needed help, but as it turned out he was unable to go so I got to know him after all. He had been a Tracker up in White Horse and the Yukon Territory most of his married life but he and my Aunt had finally returned to their roots. Vancouver Island.

I also got to meet my two cousins who were polar opposites and great company too. One was based in Vancouver City and I love that place. She was the cheeky, sporty one. The other was based in Toronto but came for a visit so I was lucky to meet her.

Their ways with each other were so funny.

"Nice hair" greeted Cousin Vancouver to her sister.

"Now you just need to work on your ass!"

I remember my Uncle growling about one of his neighbours. (He talks a little like Ned Flanders from "The Simpson's" which was inadvertently funny anyway.)

Dr High Would Like To Review Your Medication

Roz Scribble

Chapter 8: Time Travel

"Everyone licks that guy's ass. Him and me just don't see eye to eye" he barked.

"Why?" Enquired Cousin Vancouver. "Coz you're down licking his ass?"
(Me on the floor, in agony from laughing).

Cousin Toronto was more cosmopolitan and scared of The Bush. She wanted to take a trip to the west coast of the island to the Hospital she was born in and I was grateful to be invited. Long Beach! Of course I had to jump fully clothed into the Pacific Ocean.

There was a bear warning and as we walked the trails she kept stopping and whispering "Did you hear something?!" 'Yes" I whispered back."You".

Because my uncle would drag me out of bed 4am to go tracking in the mornings I had become less concerned but was starting to get a little freaked by proxy.

Anyway. I was still very shy and when we reached the Hospital she thanked me for being by her side. "I'm not" I teased. "But I am right behind you."

Big trees, big mountains, living and swimming everyday in the big Sproat Lake. Wow! Swimming one day when the rain hit the ground with such thick and heavy velocity, (my uncle always described it as "Lookie here, it's like a cow peeing on a slate!) I learnt for the first time how to enjoy my own company and at the age of 28 it had taken me a while, but I had got there and it was a beautiful new life skill.

My father died, on Christmas day. I have long forgiven him, he wasn't a well man. And I am proud that he became a successful musician against all the odds.

Dr High Would Like To Review Your Medication

Roz Scribble

Chapter 8: Time Travel

I returned once more to Vancouver Island for a further 2 months and my beloved Sproat Lake, and was lucky to spend my 30th birthday there. I met all sorts of distance relations I'd never known which was wonderful.

I even got to meet a Cougar! Black Bears were everywhere but I had met people who had spent their lives in Canada and never seen a Cougar so it was an incredible privilege.

My uncle had been called by the Ranger. A Cougar had been stalking some Logger-men and could he go chase it back up into the mountains. I still have the photo on my wall today and remember this collective silence as I, my uncle and the Logger-men stared at this amazing creature with a mixture of fear and deep respect. They are truly dignified and incredible animals.

There were more adventures to come. I had always dreamt of going to India and I finally did a year or so later as I was invited by friends living in Delhi. Never so scared in my life, I simply had to go! It was a long time ambition, and I just about made it out alive.

That first visit to India was probably the biggest, stupidest risk I have ever taken and had I been my mother I would have been worried sick. A daughter with a severe psychiatric diagnosis going off to Delhi to live with a bunch of guys she'd met off the Internet! Yet it remains one of my happiest memories.

Note to readers: *Not a recommended risk!*

Dr High Would Like To Review Your Medication

Roz Scribble

Chapter 8: Time Travel

The thing about my mother is she is open minded. One of a few Buddhists I have known that walk the talk (rather than argue about it on Facebook for 6 hours a day).
I know her secrets and she knows mine. She is like an angel that lost her wings so very young, yet no one thought to stop and ask her how she came to lose them. Well I did, and I love her all the more.

India is not the stereotype people often thinks she is. She is immensely diverse on so many levels and even by the time I reached customs and immigration I felt I had found my second home. When people invite you into their homes, you become family.

When I finally arrived at my friends place it consisted of two small rooms with no real plumbing and no kitchen. The bathroom simply had an Indian style toilet and a bucket and tap. It was on the 5th floor and I could stand on the balcony or rooftop and enjoy a panoramic view of this densely populated city.

The guys were all from up North. Hindustani men and I was always chaperoned. I respected their concerns and sense of responsibility to make sure I was safe, and I didn't want to turn that responsibility into a burden.

My dear friend took me to the famous Market that had been so horrifically bombed only a year earlier and told me how he had survived as he had had to run a last minute errand.

We also had what became known as "The Incredible Rooftop Party" and sat up enjoying the night air and the city view, giggling away until daybreak.

I then travelled North to meet my friends parents and other family. My second family.

Dr High Would Like To Review Your Medication

Roz Scribble

Chapter 9: 85 Percent is Normal

Okay So you are diagnosed with a psychosis. Psychiatric Sectarianism. It's the other side of the "Peace Wall". The stigma comes from your innermost circle including health professionals in both the private and public sector. It makes it all so much worse. Every idea is taken literally. One can't even say "I'd murder for a cup of tea" in case some Doc assumes one is homicidal. Take a pill Doc, it's only an idiom!

Then I struck gold. I met The BM Himself. (Sometimes affectionately called Yoda). A close friend to this day he ran a course and marched into the room with a loud clap of his hands and boomed,

"IS CHANGE POSSIBLE?!"

Hands wavered at varying altitudes yet by the end of the first day I realised 85 percent of all my crazy thinking was exactly the same structure of thinking we all do. What a relief! I had potential and I was going to make the most of this.

I had the opportunity to build my own box of tricks and I could use whenever necessary. If negative habitual thoughts kept appearing I could deliberately install new software in my head with just a little practise. I already knew it was my job to do the work. I just didn't know how. And that is why as I said before when people ask me if I am a "What" or a "Why" person I simply reply I am a "How" person.

Dr High Would Like To Review Your Medication

Roz Scribble

Chapter 9: 85 Percent is Normal

I sensed a window of opportunity and leapt right through it with the fervency of Father Jack from the comedy series Father Ted, only without his disparaging fear of nuns.

I decided to volunteer. This time with a seasoning of disadvantageous nervousness. I facilitated Art and Jewellery making to stoic and hilarious people suffering with terrible disabilities. I was so impressed with their humour and togetherness I always went home in a good mood. I remained there for three years.

I plucked up the courage to spend a couple of months volunteering in The Maldives, which to this day remains one of my happiest memories. Not only was I living in home stay with a generous family. My main job was simply to play with the children and snorkel on my days off on the coral reefs. I immediately took up SCUBA on my return to Ireland. A dive with a playful Seal one day in the Strangford Lough remains a favourite.

There were so many funny and humbling moments.
The time I thought I was an adventurer yet managed to get lost on an island less than half a mile square. A time I free dived off the abyss at the edge of a stunning Coral Reef and a Giant Sea Turtle whizzed by. The fish that looked as if they contained light bulbs. The nine hour boat ride to my local island at night when a small child said "shhhhhh! The fish are sleeping!" The shop keeper who spoke no English as most didn't, yet collapsed in giggles when I informed him I needed flip-flops for some very big flat feet.

Dr High Would Like To Review Your Medication

Roz Scribble

Chapter 9: 85 Percent is Normal

I am afraid this is where I engage in a rant: One of the most paradoxical things about discrimination I have experienced is that it comes from the very people who you trust. The people who are there to protect you. Your family, friends, Doctors, CPN's, Social Workers, the Police, and the Government itself. This is a multi context issue. Take Racism for example. I find it utterly pathetic.

Hypothetical:
"Can I play with you guys?"
"NO!"
"Why not?" *(saddened little intimidated face)*.
"YOU wear blue shoes. And your HAIR!"
"What?" *(confusion and tears now)*.
"WE don't play with people who wear blue shoes and have brown hair!!!"
Racism is pure childishness. We all bleed red blood. Yet we have this "Not on my turf" mentality. Sort that *Beep out in the playground, grow up and move on. It has no place in the real world. Yes it's a very simplistic analogy but...
Forms arrive at my house. "Black, White or Other"?
Christian, Protestant or "Other".

That is oversimplification. I don't want to get into serious trouble so I just write "White Titanium, Cadmium Red and varying degrees of Yellow Ochre". Those are the basic colours used to mix skin tone. What business is it of yours? From the beginnings of advocacy in Bedlam I now hug closely the image of Martin Luther King for inspiring Advocates in *every* Rights Movement to stand up (or sit rightfully on your own bus seat).

We Crazy Folk took inspiration from the Civil Rights Movement and now are just beginning to implement *Peer* Advocates in Loony Hotels to protect the Human Rights of the Clients and empower *them* to stand up for themselves. And minorities are very discriminated against in Psychiatry. I have been myself, in both the NHS and private sector. I imagine to my best ability what it must be like for black Americans being shot. Gay bashing. Islamaphobia. The media portrayal of the gentle people of India. The list is endless.

Dr High Would Like To Review Your Medication

Roz Scribble

Chapter 9: 85 Percent is Normal

The sound of the Call to Prayer occurred several times every day in the Maldives, and hypnotised me into the deepest bliss. I used to sit on the hard bathroom floor, head bowed as I soaked in this sound, the sound of pure trance and beauty.

I often listen to The Quran at night and it doesn't matter to me that I don't speak Arabic. It permits me to drift and gives me a warm safety. Like an enormous soft hand to fall asleep on.. Yet people were pleading with me not to think badly of them.

Why should they have to apologise to me? The people of the Maldives are Sunni Muslims and some of the most gentle people I have ever met. And our Spokespersons, the people running this precarious gossamer world have the arrogance to speak on my behalf?

I say the same about India, where my second family live. I got sick. I was in hospital. They held Hindu prayer vigils. They covered my face in spices on the festival of Holi, in my hospital bed. They care. I went to the temple to express gratitude. I carry them in my heart forever. I miss them terribly.

I was teaching a Driver in Goa Irish idioms and we got lost. He was giggling so much we nearly crashed twice. He refused to charge me a fare for laughing. That is human connectivity, a basic human need. The lack of alienation I have experienced in South Asia fills my heart.

Dr High Would Like To Review Your Medication

Roz Scribble

Chapter 9: 85 Percent is Normal

I bought some Black Musk Oil from the United Arab Emirates. The smell reminds me of Indian Markets and I can go there in my head any time I like. I have a truckload of little tricks that are more helpful than any pill or injection I have been given.

No problem. Self validate at will. I am the one with the smile on my face...

Eventually my volunteering turned to helping out a little on courses with people suffering from Depression to young Ex-Cons, which I see as equally incapacitating. Once I had heard the stories of these people any judgements I was unaware of came to the surface and evaporated due to sheer lack of necessity.

If I learnt someone was a vandal I understood how they came to feel so disaffected. I became much more open minded regarding every behaviour.

As a society we judge the effects of people's behaviour yet pay little attention to the causality and torment behind it. I simply want to help. Not because I believe I am great and full of gems of wisdom but because I believe I have empathy and insight into various behaviours.

I went on to study quite a few therapeutic models. Partly as self help, and partly with the ambition to help others, including Peer Advocacy.

Then one day I made a huge and almighty mistake.

Dr High Would Like To Review Your Medication

Roz Scribble

Chapter 9: 85 Percent is Normal

I was in Goa alone and stupidly leapt into a river of elephants. A tourist trap. I still wonder what part of me didn't think 'Um... Water borne infection?'!

I was sicker than a worn out Delhi Street Dog and taking 25-30 Imodium per day. The local Doctor had me on insane amounts of Nitrazepam for the muscle cramps, I was as high as a runaway kite. I still have little recollection of how I managed the 5 Airports it took to reach home.

10 days in bed. 10 days of my poor mother begging me to go to A&E. Eventually I lost the power of speech due to severe dehydration and was rushed to an isolation unit. Apparently it was a very rare strain of South East Asian Salmonella. And it would take two and a half years of internal bleeding to resolve.

I lost count of the courses of IV's and the courses of antibiotics. I'm told my veins are lumpy now. Nurses sometimes have to take routine blood tests from my hands. Nobody warned me my mind was at risk and I became disaffected with people in the Public and Private sector. Some that marketed themselves as so called Mental Health Experts when their knowledge was merely cerebral, and insight was plain dreadful.

I suffered hideous long term memory loss. I lost count of the near death experiences, comas, vomiting/ passing blood and passing out, needles, Biopsy's, radiology and internal cameras etc…

I was tired of cantankerous bullies. I felt disillusioned that I didn't know the answers and ill-affected that apparently neither did anyone else when everyone seemed to be an expert. I was sick of everyone and everything, and deeply traumatised.

Dr High Would Like To Review Your Medication

Roz Scribble

Chapter 11: In the Maldives...

Lets step back from all that. I must have been completely balmy. Years prior to Goa I sensed a window of adventure readiness. A sense of wellness. I decided it was time to take a big risk again. I was in part giving the finger to the Psychiatrist who told me my life would never amount to anything.

I decided to volunteer overseas. Expensive, and you need to be a Doctor or Nurse or qualified teacher. Yet I found an organisation based in the Maldives that looked possible, and I scrimped and saved.

I wrote to them and was completely upfront. I thought they would said not on your life! I basically told them I was Mentally unwell, on reams of medication most of which isn't even prescribed in the Maldives and probably had the worst employment history of any applicant. For some reason they seemed to appreciate my honesty and went out of their way to help me as long as I got a Police Disclosure check and two character references.

I didn't know if I was capable. I just knew I was in my mid 30's, short on adventure and good memories, and it was the only way I would not only get to see this stunning country but live with the locals. (It's illegal for tourists to visit those islands except on excursions where they are shuffled like penguins and not allowed to deviate from the group).

I couldn't tell the difference between fear or excitement. Many gap year students go there on Daddy's money but for me it would be the opportunity of a lifetime.

Dr High Would Like To Review Your Medication

Roz Scribble

Chapter 11: In the Maldives...

I actively hate flying. It is not fear of crashing. It is the relentless tedium. And it was a very long flight. But two very exciting things happened I had not witnessed before.

Flying over Oman at night I witnessed two absolutely enormous thunderstorms collide underneath slightly north of our flight and I was pressed against the glass in absolute fascination. Then later I noticed to the left of the window was night and to the right was dawn. Probably the only time I have been excited on a plane. Planes usually remind me of Mental Hospitals, only with marginally better behaviour.

The plane landed on a man-made landing strip that starts on the Indian Ocean and finishes just as abruptly at the ocean too. As the cabin door opened the heat poured in and I realised it was so close to the equator I was going to spend most of my time drenched with sweat. (Something the locals enjoyed teasing me about).

The most turquoise water I had ever seen and the compulsion to run down the steps off the plane just to leap fully clothed into the sea was almost overwhelming.

Two queues at immigration. Tourist or work Visas. I didn't understand so I approached a guard who took my papers and appeared a few minutes later and led me right past all the queues much to the disgust of everyone else. My luggage was soaked. I learnt later they fumigate due to a horrifying plague of Black Widow Spiders a few years earlier.

Dr High Would Like To Review Your Medication

Roz Scribble

Chapter 11: In the Maldives...

Two days and one night on the Capital Island Male and the founder of the organisation was like an adorable sister and hooked me up with the coolest tour guide. I went to see a temple, but it was closed yet a generous Iman gave me lots of educational books translated into English for free.

My hotel adjoined a cafe and the boys were always joking and friendly, nicknaming me "The Story Teller" as I was journaling everything that made me giggle.

Then the following night I got a Sea Taxi. I had to board by a sliding plank whilst assertively slapping away the hands of my would be rescuers in preparation for the 9 hour boat ride to my Island. These local sea taxis have been converted from fishing vessels and the passenger area upstairs is around four feet in height. I spent the 9 hours outside on deck in the darkest atmosphere I have ever seen with my legs dangling over the edge of the boat. My bones were in agony after a while from the hard floor.

A charming man told me his life story and explained the experience of the Boxing day Tsunami. His recollection of events made me feel freezing cold all of a sudden, and I could only imagine the terror as he explained the sequence of events and the confusion as none on his island knew what a tsunami was. I was entranced, with a mixture of attraction and empathy, my head spinning with imagination.

I played with a small and highly entertaining child for a while. I fended off some sex deprived man but mostly I stared peacefully at the awe inspiring pitch black Indian Ocean, save distant lights from the occasional Island or passing ship. I have never experienced vast darkness like that before or since.

Dawn broke and I could see the Island I was to live on grow in perspective as we approached the shore. Suddenly I felt wrecked, tired and very, very shy.

Dr High Would Like To Review Your Medication

Roz Scribble

Chapter 11: In the Maldives...

The Lady of the House I was to live in was waiting for me and I greeted her with a sort of exhausted maniacal grin. Grandma was adorable and spoke no English but we make friends the usual way. Comedy hand signals.

"You must sleep immediately" commanded TLoTH. "There is an Independence Parade tonight and you will attend".

I thought I could sleep for days as she showed me to my room. My very own room! I must have been judgemental as I wasn't expecting that. I was warned it would be basic but I had a powerful ceiling fan and my very own bathroom with a tap high in the wall with cold desalinated sea water to pour on me every time I needed to cool down. My gosh. Coming from snow-ridden Northern Ireland I never did adjust to the climate. It took two days for my clothes to dry even in the blinding sun due to the humidity and there rarely seemed a sea breeze.

There was a Tsunami warning during my stay. I felt stabs of anxiety and then abject guilt when I learnt of the devastation in Japan.

There were two volunteers when I arrived. One left due to culture shock and the other left in a highly paranoid huff. So I felt I managed fine. The first to leave commented to the Minister of Education for the Atoll, "Nice day today".
Then added hastily, "As usual..."

We fell about laughing.

Dr High Would Like To Review Your Medication

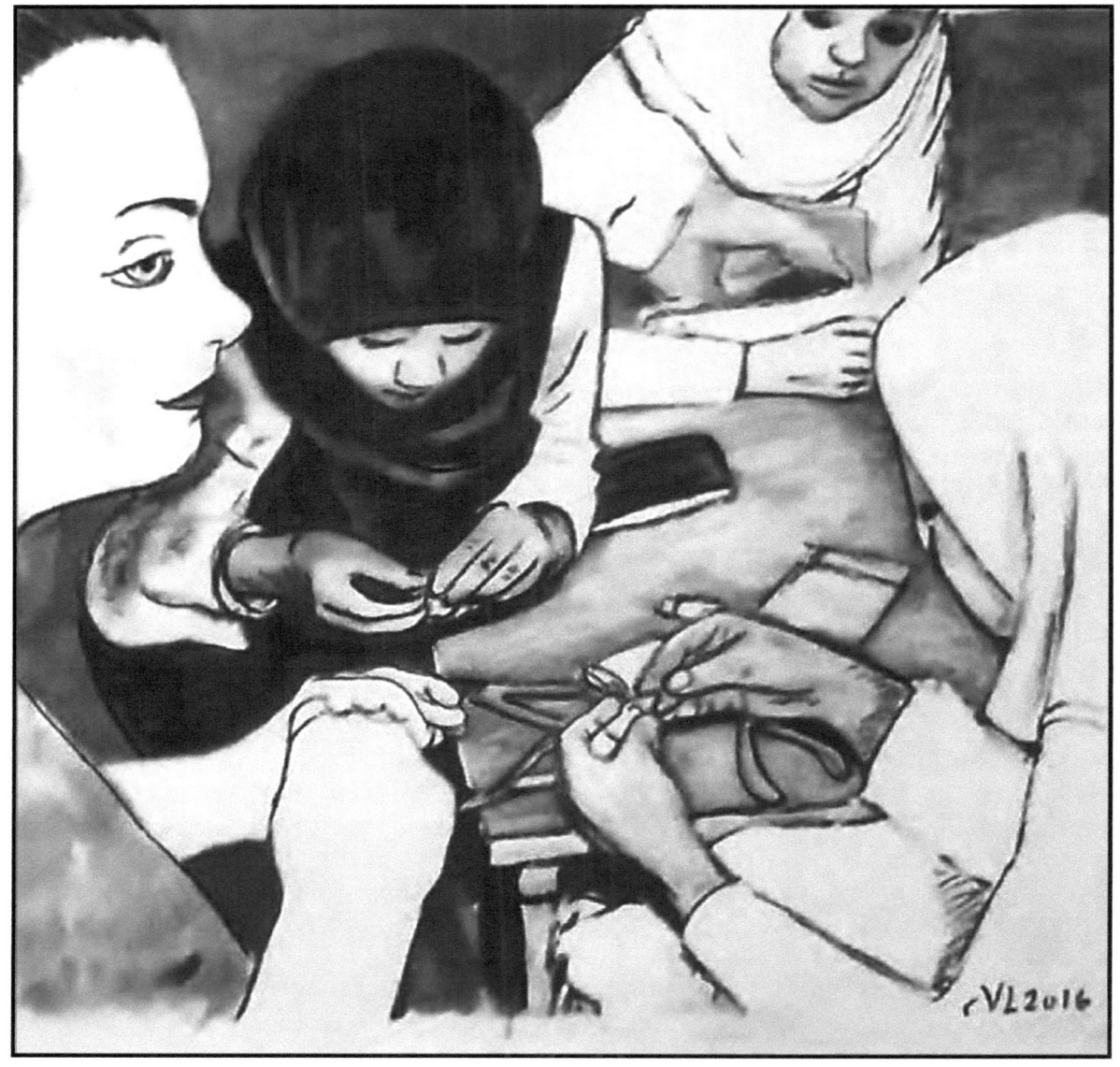

Roz Scribble

Chapter 11: In the Maldives...

First day at the school. I got lost. It's pretty typical of me but even I didn't think I could get lost on an Island almost one third of a mile square.
It didn't help that a 3 year old girl took one look at me and promptly burst into tears.

The women are so pretty I felt like a big clumsy Orang-utan and managed to break out in some kind of heat rash all over my face prompting another 3 year old being sent to the Principal's office in distress.

Now moved to the class of 5 year olds, the teacher spoke no English. She seemed angry with the children a lot (they were a little naughty, and seeing me as the Novelty Aunty they really took advantage). I drew them lots of pictures to colour in to distract them. One day a teacher walked in and I was building a staircase out of Lego, completely oblivious that the children had run off. *How embarrassing!*

I always thought it was very sweet that the children thought I was from India and would point at the sky as if that meant North. They really were adorable.

I did find it strange though that they had a sand pit in the playground. The whole island was sand! And there was a huge Banyan Tree by the school and one lunch hour I counted 40 sleeping Fruit Bats before giving up. Teddy bears with big wings! I grew a love of Geckos, all kinds of lizards, and their little night time light bulb parties.

Dr High Would Like To Review Your Medication

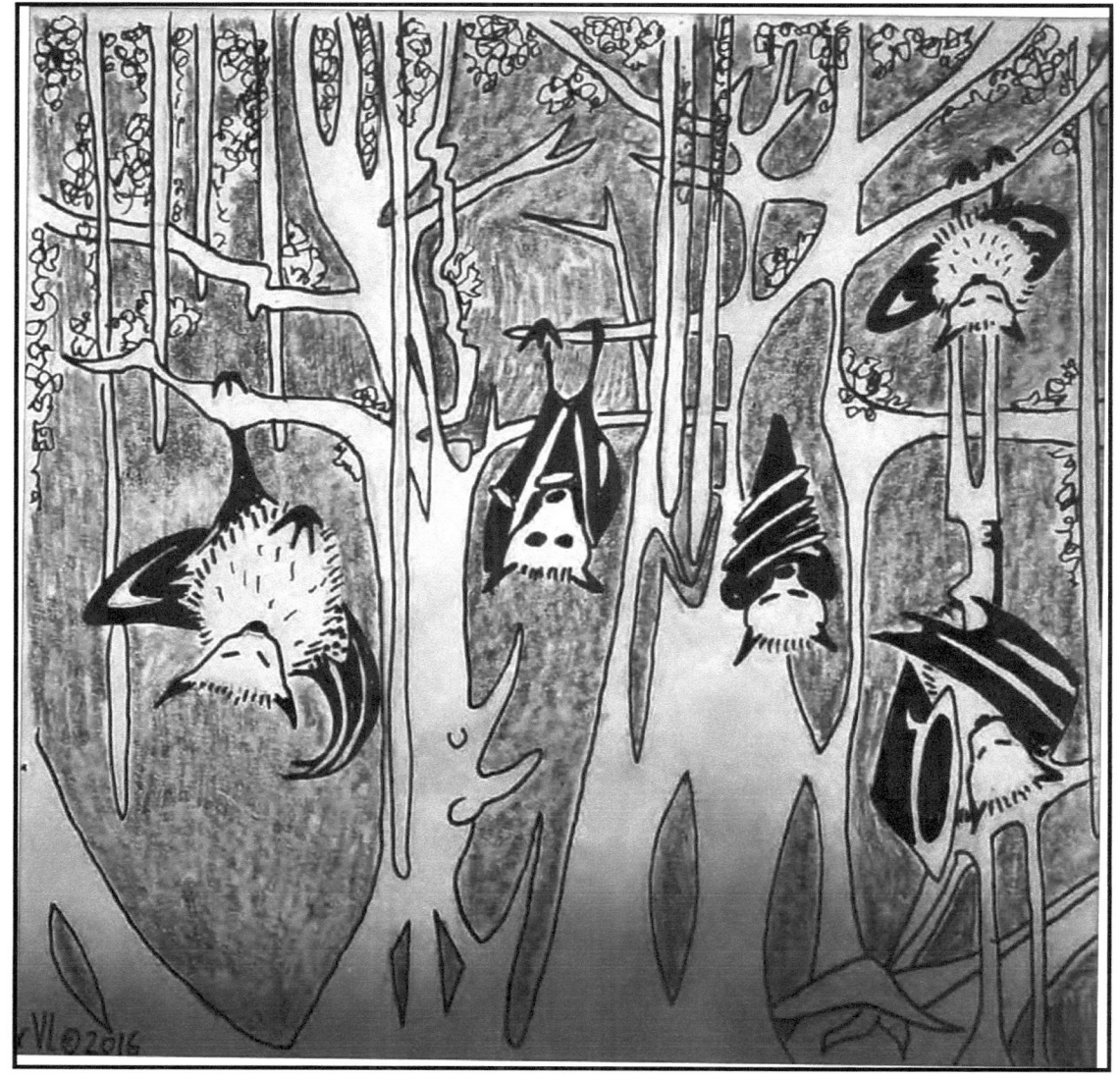

Roz Scribble

Chapter 11: In the Maldives...

There seemed to be various disabilities on the Island and no real facilities. I was highly impressed to see one man had fashioned a seat with three thick tires and placed bicycle pedals as handlebars scooting around merrily. There were other difficulties I simply hadn't seen before and was glad to see no discrimination. The island was one big family.

People wandered in and out of other people's houses and it was social like that. I didn't know who lived where. I think for the locals not much happened. I mean the excitement when a very obese man was riding on the back on another man's Scooter and the tyre burst! The Scooter owner shouted at him, but the Islanders were laughing for hours.

The Police were great. They didn't seem to have much to do. Unfortunately my rucksack got stolen with my money and passport and with no British Embassy in The Maldives they had to send a report to Sri Lanka. Eventually I became so impatient with the police officer I basically wrote the report myself.

I knew what wasn't in my rucksack. My happiness and my adventure and I was not going to give it away so I shrugged it off and kept my spirits high.

The Minister of Education for the Atoll was so generous he gave me a wad of cash! The only thing that upset me was the elders pleading with me not to think badly of Muslims and persuading me they were a peaceful people. I didn't need persuading. I loved them.

Dr High Would Like To Review Your Medication

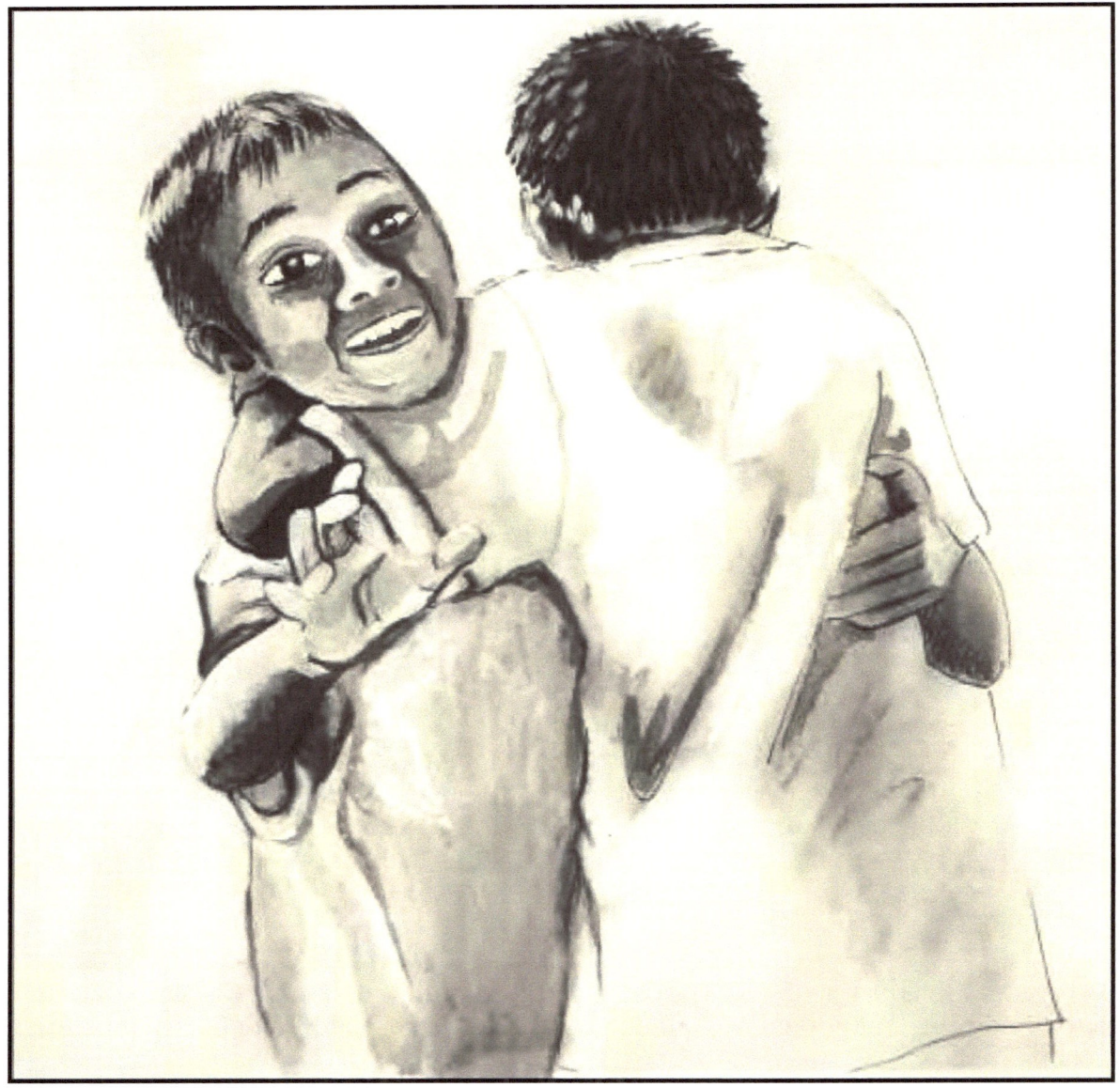

Roz Scribble

Chapter 11: In the Maldives...

It is such fun being in a country when you don't speak the language. If two people were having an argument I just named them "Voice 1" and "Voice 2". It was very easy to work out by the tonality and cadence who was winning.

Their first local Council elections happened during my stay and as "Voice 1" spoke in measured slow confident tones and maintained that decorum I realised it was as much in the delivery as the rhetoric. "Voice 2" metamorphosed into a desperate rapid high pitched appeal and it merely increased in desperation so I knew he had lost.

It was the same with a husband and wife next door. She had the same consistency and his voice transformed into a guttural decline. He lost. Badly.

The evening of the Elections I was invited to a "Special Celebration" and chairs lined the sea front. To my absolute bafflement a huge Russian man in full Tuxedo appeared and proceeded to sing "My Way" in an Operatic voice. Was it a dream? The result was my falling about laughing uncontrollably, but fortunately he seemed to take it as a complement, winking. It was so very surreal.

The mosque next to me had the opposite effect. I even bought a CD of the Quran when I got back as it helps me sleep. I was lucky that the Iman had a stunning peaceful voice and I very much miss that sense of stillness every time the call to prayer came.

Dr High Would Like To Review Your Medication

Roz Scribble

Chapter 11: In the Maldives...

A new experience. I guess for some of the islanders The Maldives is all they have ever known, excepting husbands who work away from home and I had a hard job persuading people to come and spend a day on an uninhabited island with me.

Eventually TLoTH's cousin took me by boat to a stunning jungle island with one elderly caretaker living in a tin hut there. It was absolutely stunning. They had made a little clearing to grow lemons and Mangoes etc. as local produce tends to be limited to Bread Fruit (which the Fruit Bats love) and of course coconuts. Most things are imported hence a Doctor costing the same as a bottle of Juice.

I snorkelled and snorkelled and saw colours I have never seen before and fish that seemed lit from inside, it blew my mind. The highlight was a giant Sea Turtle whizzing past me, as I fought my own buoyancy to free dive deep into the abyss past the coral reef.

I had a brief moment close to tears when I realised it would soon become just a memory, but shoved the thought aside and simply felt like the luckiest person in the world.

I did cry in private when eventually it was time to return home. But as we know, one day The Maldives will disappear and I am so exceptionally fortunate to have had such an incredible experience. I still think fondly of my friends and adopted family.

Dr High Would Like To Review Your Medication

Roz Scribble

Diagnosis Criminal & The 8 Day Migraine

I developed a severe migraine, and was prescribed a mere 75mg of aspirin, 1x every 24 hours. So I phoned the Health Centre to see if it was a mistake.

I explained "I have a severe migraine and it's..."
"No" the Doctor interrupted firmly. "What makes you think you have a Migraine?"

Good Grief! He was parroting me during our little chat on the phone as if he had just attended an Adult Night School in Counselling Skills, level 1. And I mean on the first night, having dropped out after the first break!

"I am diagnosed with migraines, I know the symptoms".

I was paying close attention to my breathing, took two breaths as a Life Coach from New York had taught me, rolling my eyes upwards to a sense of calm and responded, "And what makes you think I have intermittent headaches?" (Parrot me? Parrot you.)
"Because it says so right here on the Hospital Report."
"The Hospital Report is incorrect" I responded calmly. "I have had a migraine for nearly a week."
"Well" he insisted in a non-negotiable manner. "I have given you my professional opinion".
"Do you realise the paramedic, the out of hours doctor and the staff at the Pharmacy think you are nuts too?"
"I want their names if you have them."
[What?!!!]
"Would you be prioritising a personal vendetta over patient care, Doctor?" [Silence...]
"Thank you for your time Doctor. Goodbye"
[click]

Dr High Would Like To Review Your Medication

Roz Scribble

Diagnosis Criminal & the 8 Day Migraine

I was livid. Not with Christmas. With my Health Centre. Then I did what I should have done in the first place. Booked a state registered private Physiotherapist. The migraine eased to a headache by the end of the session, and though it returned I notified her and she emailed me some tailor made stretches and videos. Problem solved.

I applied to a new Health Centre; but not before writing to the practise manager and explaining that I was diagnosing 2 of the doctors with a condition called "Hierarchical Grandiosity". (Yep, I made it up, my DSM alternative). Take 75mg of Reality, 1x every 24 hours and drink plenty of fluids.
Emails had been sent to them by a kid I'd clashed with. Emails I had no recollection of due to being half dead, literally, and some major falsification was involved but it was months later that I learnt the extent of it. With no memory I was defenceless.

Suddenly syringes appeared and the following day my neck had swollen to twice it's normal size and body was behaving as if it had developed a fully developed and accelerated form of Tardive Dyskinesia, which gave me that semi rigour mortice look so obvious in Psychiatric Hospitals.

Fuming, my mother told me everything the Health Centre had hidden, as a member of staff had told her everything, and I do mean everything, but to keep it from me. I immediately wrote to my GP, and was subsequently stonewalled. They wriggled their way out of the neglect and discrimination they had employed.

Then, as if things could get any worse, I was approached by "The Force "and when I say that, I do not mean Star Wars!

Dr High Would Like To Review Your Medication

Roz Scribble

Diagnosis Criminal & The 8 Day Migraine

A little blond constable have turned up at the door, and to be fair she was more Compassionate Nurse than Cop Shop. Why do people call it the "Cop Shop"? I'm not buying it. Anyway she told me what I had apparently done and I had no choice but to accept it.

I was never put in a car, hand on my head as they do. Never handcuffed. Never put in a cell.

The CBT Guy actually got it. He nailed it and we examined what evidence we had, the result being he was one of only a few with the intelligence to realise I was severely unwell, threatened via email and my reaction was most certainly not the sum total of my parts and even somewhat logical under the circumstances.

The story given to the Police was embellished and with the odd lie thrown in, and the statement typically strategic. I even got so upset about all this one night I emailed the following cartoon to my local police as a "present". My fist was almost stuffed in my mouth the following morning in a state of 'Yikes! *What* did I just do!'

Anyway, through the long haul, most people were generally very nice.

Dr High Would Like To Review Your Medication

Roz Scribble

Chapter 11: The Out of Hours Phenomenon

You know the old ones from people who don't experience this.
'Pull your socks up!'. 'What makes you so special?'. [Yawn].

Next time someone gives you a hard time it's probably easier if you just draw them a picture. Or a great deal faster if you nod, smile and confuse them.

Obviously very specific things happen inside the body when you panic, or go to the extremes of a "Panic Attack". I have heard people make judgements regarding calling it an "attack". That is what it is like.

Most people here have heard of 'Fight or Flight'. A perfectly normal reaction to danger. The majority of the time we are not in life threatening situations though. Alas the Physiology remains and when it becomes so extreme that it stops one's ability to function it's considered pathological..

To prepare for the danger you run or defend yourself. Symptoms include a rapid heart and a sudden inexplicable sense of danger and confusion. It's terrifying. You may feel utterly terrified with the need to leave the area immediately (flight). The adrenaline can make us lose control of our limbs. The palpitations can make us fear we will have a heart attack.

Your circulation speeds up and pumps blood to increase oxygen to enable you to respond to the danger by making a decision.

Example: I used to get terrible stage fright on Piano. You don't need your hands to run so the blood pumps away from them to your vital organs and it's like trying to play with a bunch of bananas on the end of each arm.

Dr High Would Like To Review Your Medication

Roz Scribble

Chapter 11: The Out of Hours Phenomenon

Sometimes little things happen to exacerbate the symptoms.

This is the Weekends. When Mental [ill] Health patients (or anyone in poor health really) feel agitated, afraid and left to rot if an emergency should occur and they can seem to last forever.

A long, long time ago I dreaded them. Where do you turn to when absolutely desperate for medical assistance and there is little "Care in the Community", other than an Out of Hours Doctor (who won't visit your house in a million years).

Because this made the symptoms a million times worse I nick-named it 'The Out Of Hours Phenomenon' as this is what happens, and I'm sure every Nurse/ Doctor and so on has noticed because there will be a sudden inexplicable Rush Hour 30 minutes before closing time on a Friday night.

It right back to that simple trigger of the thought of it. Oh my gosh, what will happen *if*? One weekend I was having the Mother of all Panic Attacks and couldn't seem to help myself at all. I knew there would be a queue of very sick people. People worse off. People needing defibrillators. Feeling ashamed and full of guilt I phoned anyway.

He was pleasant and said to come over to the Community Hospital and he'd leave an envelope with something to calm me down. (How he thought I was going to actually get there possibly bypassed his thinking), but fortunately my ever helpful mother ran me there. Phew! Crisis would soon be over. But all that was there was a little brown envelope with a single 2mg tablet of Diazepam in it.

Kind of the equivalent of attempting to increase fish stocks by chucking a Viagra off the end of a pier.

Yay. I just got humoured!

Dr High Would Like To Review Your Medication

Roz Scribble

Chapter 11: The Out of Hours Phenomenon

I don't know exactly how old I was. Probably 5 or 6 at the most. At that that time the grocers was just up the road, and my mother liked to give my twin and I small errands to run with nice clear instructions on paper and a little purse with change in it.

I stared with dead eyes at our front gates. Back in those days Agoraphobia was still defined as fear of wide open spaces. But these days it's considered more a sense of impending doom that becomes so extreme you can become a prisoner in your own home.

I didn't want to go, I never wanted to do these things even though my twin was with me. Something really bad was going to happen! It would involve a very angry man. I let my sister take charge and shakily managed to get up there and back with her lead. I think that sort of established our pecking order for life.

This is my earliest memory of something that would eventually become severe Agoraphobia. In the future there would be many occasions where I didn't leave the house for months on end. Years sometimes,
without someone with me.

It's very common. A lot of people find it worse in crowds (shopping malls etc.) and the usual intervention is exposure. Either by the deep end or by gentle and slowly paddling out to the water's edge and dipping one toe in repeatedly.

Just like my Panic Attack on the London Underground it can be very humiliating and the main plan is to get to safety and solitude as fast as is humanly possible.

Dr High Would Like To Review Your Medication

Roz Scribble

Chapter 14: Self Harm from the Horse's Mouth

I want to touch briefly on the subject of Self Harm. There is much mythology. There is an enormous world of difference between the actual experience of a Self Harmer and the imposed theorising by Therapists, Doctors, lay persons and the perspective of the individual concerned.

This terrifying and tragic world the sufferer resides in is has now been discussed more widely and even more importantly the need for direct input from Self Harmer's has finally been recognised as a fundamental requirement to help others in similar circumstances and clinicians alike.

Self harm comes in a multitude of forms. People in the western hemisphere often cut their arms, especially adolescents and that is the usual perception of a self-harmer, but there are many patterns and adults engage in this too. Other examples include driving at full speed into a wall, swallowing enough pills to cause unconsciousness but not death. (Accidental suicides can occur under those circumstances.) Alcohol and other narcotics, smashing oneself repeated against a wall or mirror.

It also varies geographically. In some countries people will drink bleach. There are endless approaches but the one thing they all have in common is the immediate need to stop the way the person is thinking and feeling by any means possible which is exactly why the label "Self Harming" is a bit of an oversimplification.

I have witnessed severe life threatening Self Harm too, but often it is important too to recognise that Self Harming is also a Negative Coping Strategy for specific reasons, hence the relief it brings to the harmer and the dangerously addictive nature of it.

Dr High Would Like To Review Your Medication

Roz Scribble

Chapter 14: Self Harm from the Horse's Mouth

I have no recollection of how I became a "Self Harmer". I know I was around 14 years old. The idea didn't fall out of the sky and I don't recall anyone else I knew doing this. It was before the majority of people had computers never mind social networking yet I must have learnt about it from somewhere because I did it in variants. As I watched the visual effects and felt the familiar release of endorphins from my brain sooth my mental anguish it was if I had found I was paradoxically able to nurture myself. My tears stopped, my body relaxed and the following morning I had experienced the deepest sleep.
I have learnt now human contact and nurture is fundamental and book Indian Head Massages for these needs. Also remember this. Thoughts are temporary, yet physical scars remain.

It took years to break the habit, like drug withdrawal. How else to channel emotions? I learnt that in reality, I need meaning and purpose to survive. If you think Self Harming is merely "attention seeking" you are naive and need a (metaphorical) slap.

An external form of harm is the label "You are mentally ill". Please feel free to disagree, it is only an opinion. I fundamentally oppose the notion Psychosis is a disease. Events in childhood can affect our self concepts destructively. Triggers later on can cause symptoms. I doubt it is a neurological disease and though yes, it is hard wired in our brains it is a Trauma. We can get better with appropriate resources and practise. Pills are risky and if they help they certainly do not address the underlying thinking and behaviours.

We need to normalise Mental Illness as it is so common it should not be so taboo.

Roz Scribble

Chapter 14: The Beginning

Just over a year after I was cautioned by the police my diagnosis was in question again. One very lengthy experience with Schizophrenia but they now felt it could be Psychological Trauma instead, and it explained why the previous two and a half years of internal bleeding had caused me to go utterly and completely bonkers. Stacked Traumas.

It was now so obvious, and the change in my behaviour when I was struck down with Long Term Salmonella began to make sense. I realised I had been carrying resentment my whole life and it became so heavy I had no choice but to drop it. But in the mental and physical state I was in I dropped it in the wrong place, on other people. And more crucially, the only people I had dropped it on was people I were deeply afraid of. I had come to this realisation one day while sitting in my mother's kitchen. I went into a state of complete and utter panic and began shaking violently. I had been too cantankerous for my own values to a small number of people and now that I had seen the light I realised that at last the process of recovery had begun.

I had a job to do now and it was crucial that I worked very hard to build emotional resilience and forgiveness of myself and others. People I had knocked off the very pedestal I myself placed them on in the first place, hence the extreme fear.

I had been sick of all these people coming down on me like a ton of bricks. (Well I did knock them off those pedestals. They rained down on me.) That makes a person's head hurt. It is why I had an 8 day Migraine. Metaphors had triggered the pain receptors in my brain. It is why some of them launched vicious counter attacks.

I started to become less afraid of my own emotions, as I gained some understanding and even began to respect negative experience and see the benefits of usefully channelled emotion, anger that generates motivation for example. I was lucid and ready to work hard. My behaviour began to change rapidly and I was able to begin taking action again.

Dr High Would Like To Review Your Medication

Roz Scribble

Chapter 14: The Beginning

I had been expressing my experience of ill health directly through my behaviour, without modifying it for the purposes of social norms, hence I was considered weird, mad, bad, and subsequently dehumanised. I had held resentment about this but I now realised that it was an important message in my environment and I began paying attention and taking responsibility.

Pleased to be receiving help from my Psychiatrist again, I drew a line in the sand, and planted the past in a metaphorical rubbish bin.

I had been seeing Psychiatrists since the age of 14 and was often disaffected being in that role. Utterly perplexed. I had been viewing my life through other people's perspectives.

Choices:
1 - Give up and die.
2 - Settle for a mediocre existence.
3 - Learn everything I possibly could from everything that happened. I chose number three.

I am glad to know the difference between a belief and a fact and have a thirst to always learn. Some People Helpers have taught me so much. The BM Himself gave me some fabulous advice. To be congruent and authentic and treat people with respect, and that they would throw it right back at me. He was right.

Many things I find useful have nothing to do with Psychiatry or Therapy. Art, Volunteering, Education, Music and Travel for example teach team work and creative living.

My passions have rekindled and I am somewhere else entirely. It has been an absolute joy studying varied subjects from Art to NLP and Advocacy. I have met some of the funniest and incredible people who have inspired me. When trouble is afoot I now walk away.

Dr High Would Like To Review Your Medication

Roz Scribble

Chapter 14: The Beginning

I know we can change, and that requires doing the work ourselves. You wouldn't expect someone else to walk your weight off.

And the importance of building relationships with people who need assistance, and helping them resourcefully can be a reciprocal relationship. Helping their loved ones to adjust and accept their changes is equally vital.

I live in a beautiful new home away from dangerous people and write and paint and draw as I look through my window at the trees. It doesn't matter if it is any good. It is that spirit of child's plays that is important to nourish.

People have often asked me if Art imitates life or Life imitates Art. We tend to separate the two as we do with work and play, yet it is both. When we combine that child's plays with the skills of an adult we have a work of Art, and that is a good philosophy for living.

I learnt in the Maldives not to give my adventure and happiness away to those who are disparaging. I learnt in Canada to engage with myself and enjoy my own company. India taught me true friendship. Sometimes I do forget. But like swimming or riding a bike it never leaves us. We can bring around these resources again and discover new ones, especially when coming to terms with adversity.

Dr High Would Like To Review Your Medication

Roz Scribble

Chapter 14: The Beginning

Psychiatry is full of nominalisations, oversimplifications and assumptions that are highly indefinite.

For those with direct experience of Mental Health issues there is a wonderful potential for helping others. The Psychotherapist's "Observer" perspective can be a good thing, but unfortunately there can be on occasion a holier than thou approach to Therapy in Psychiatry, and in Private Therapy, as the inferences have a tendency to rely on concepts of a metaphorical nature that are hierarchically grandiose and sectarian.

Yet People-helpers do have to be exceptionally patient and go home, coping with their own lives, after witnessing terrible traumas and I applaud them for that when they are so underfunded and under researched. I am grateful to those who have helped.

No matter how awful things get, and how many of your inner sphere of people disappoint you, they are just muddling along too. One day by sharing your own story should you choose to do so you will inspire people to work hard and get well because you will have shown them hope and proof, and they will show others too. It is a fantastic gift you have to give.

The years after contracting rare Salmonella were the worst of my life but despite being ostracised I have grown. I have recalled some gems gifted to me by friends and people along the way.

It is one thing to play little mind games with oneself alone though, and make mini breakthroughs. It has to be applied.

Roz Scribble

Chapter 14: The Beginning

When falling apart, I kept reminding myself of the mind-body connection and how very little memory I had. I was so confused I would look at old things as if seeing them for the first time. I didn't even recognise my surroundings on occasion.

But hey. A favourite Film quote is from Papillion when Dustin Hoffman's character is talking with a fellow prisoner. He shrugs and simply says. "Blame is for God and small children".

I take from that the futility of blame. Of others and ourselves. It serves no purpose other than to stick a label on other people to avoid taking responsibility for our own issues.

Just because "other groups" are considered normal doesn't make them so different from us. They just haven't been tossed out into Care In The Community and forgotten about. Everyone has their strife, and life is unfair no matter how you attempt to rationalise it. Everybody suffers but they deny it to the outside world.

"The World is a Stage..." Why act? It's an unwritten rule amongst a million other unwritten rules. Never show emotion in public. Never reveal the real you. We are not so different as people. Everyone suffers what there is to suffer. Everyone appreciates those precious moments.
Maybe that is why "normals'" feel they have to pretend. Fear of not being graded with a distinction in normality. Fear *is* normal.

Dr High Would Like To Review Your Medication

Roz Scribble

Chapter 14: The Beginning

I am a little critical regarding interventions in which the sole emphasis is placed on what-is-wrong.

Build attributes. Do things that actively raise self esteem with a positive attitude.

There is a paradoxical barrier, that the mistrust placed upon Mental Health patients only serves to widen the chasm of fear of Doctors, and other groups of people.

There *is* change in the air though. We are beginning to have a voice.

There isn't a person on Earth who can't be discriminated for one form or another. Too tall, too short, too thin, too posh, too common, socially eccentric etc. So if they laugh at my "condition" I may as well have a laugh at me too. And I do.

My experience of any place is an experience of the place itself. It is not merely introspective. It is a divided perspective to claim otherwise. I observe a place, as others observe me. Yet they experience the effects of my experience, not the causality, and then judge accordingly.

Maybe if more empathy was experienced for the *experience* of others, people suffering from mental health issues or indeed any issues wouldn't be so alienated.

Dr High Would Like To Review Your Medication

Roz Scribble

Chapter 15: The Beginning

This is The Beginning.

You will feel confused. Remember, "normals'" are also mixed-up. There is no handbook for negotiating this life. This world is a crazy adventure and we can learn as we feel our way along. We can expand our comfort zones as we move. Keep moving, it is crucial that we do not stagnate. If we do, we can state intentions positively. Everyone knows what they do not want, so figure out what you do want. Reclaim your passions and interests. If you don't know how, there are reams of resources and books that can assist.

If you are not diagnosed, yet traumatised by getting into any kind of trouble. There is no blame. I have met plenty of people who have been in trouble, even prison. When I have heard their stories, they have my respect and support for having survived terrible hardship in life.

Connectivity is vital for us all. Reach out to people wisely. There are good people in this world. If "Red Flags" appear exercise a simple U-turn. Conflict is hard, and unnecessary.

Your life has something to offer. Offer it with understanding and authenticity. You can help others in your own unique way. Your perceived weakness is your talent. Inspire, because you can. You have one foot on both sides of this fence of so called sanity, and that gives you the potential for a wider perspective in terms of how you experience other people's behaviour.

My deepest respect.

Dr High Would Like To Review Your Medication

www.ingramcontent.com/pod-product-compliance
Lightning Source LLC
Chambersburg PA
CBHW040905020526
44114CB00037B/58